# HOW DO I STOP STRESSING ABOUT MONEY?

## KAREN AND KEN GONYER

SMITH
FREEMAN
Publishing

# HOW DO I STOP STRESSING ABOUT MNEY?

# CONTENTS

# A MESSAGE FROM THE AUTHORS

If you're stressed about money, you're not alone. In today's easy-credit, buy-now-and-pay-later world, millions of hardworking people have been caught in a trap of debt and worry. Far too many folks struggle to make ends meet, living day to day or paycheck to paycheck. But you don't have to. You can learn to minimize stress by managing your finances carefully and well. And this book is intended to help.

On the pages that follow, you'll be asked to think about ways you can reduce stress by taking control of your money before your money—or more accurately your *lack* of money—takes control of you. You'll be reminded of fourteen common-sense strategies for proactively managing your finances. You'll be asked to take practical steps, like making a written financial plan, and you'll be asked to put the brakes on destructive behaviors, like impulsive spending. You'll also be asked to think realistically about yourself, your finances, your future, your goals, and your life. When you take these steps, you'll be more organized, more disciplined, more confident, and less stressed.

You inhabit a world in which it's harder to make

money than it is to spend it. So it's no surprise that money problems inevitably rank high on the list of common everyday stressors. But even if you're deeply in debt or deeply discouraged by your current situation, you must never lose hope. To manage money wisely, you won't need to transform yourself into a financial genius; you'll simply need to learn a few straightforward principles and apply them consistently as you confront the inevitable realities everyday life.

Over the years, we've shared common-sense financial advice with individuals, with couples, and with groups. Along the way, we've come to realize that the principles of sound money management aren't difficult to understand. In fact, most people have a general idea of the steps they need to take in order to achieve financial peace, but they simply cannot bring themselves to do the things that are required to put their financial houses in order. The key to their success is not comprehension; it's implementation. And implementation can be hard.

In the fourteen chapters of this book, we'll ask you to make a financial plan and, just as importantly, to implement it. If you take even a single idea from this text and apply it to the everyday realities of your financial life, you'll have taken an important first step. But if you can implement most or all of these fourteen strategies, you'll be surprised—and perhaps even amazed—by the stress-reducing benefits of sound money-management.

And finally, please indulge us as we address, ever so briefly, an aspect of your life that is far more important than the size of your bank balance. We're talking, of course, about your faith. We believe that God has a plan for your life, a plan that only He can see. We also believe that you and your Creator, working together, can organize your life, prioritize your duties, redirect your thoughts, and follow the path that He intends for you to take. When you do these things, you'll receive the peace and the spiritual abundance that can—and should—be yours.

So as you consider your own circumstances, remember this: whatever the size of your challenges, God is bigger. Much bigger. He will instruct you, protect you, and energize you if you let Him. So let Him. Pray fervently, listen carefully, work diligently, and treat every single day as an exercise in spiritual growth because that's precisely what every day can be—and will be—if you learn to let God lead the way.

Many blessings to you and yours,
*Ken and Karen Gonyer*

# 1

## THE QUESTION

I know that I should be doing a better
job of managing my money,
but I'm not even sure where to start.
What's the first step I should take?

## THE ANSWER

If you want to gain control over your money
and your life, you'll need to begin by
gaining a clear understanding of your current
financial situation. Once you've figured
out where you stand financially, then you
can determine where you want to go.

*We lie loudest when we lie to ourselves.*

Eric Hoffer

*You'll never find yourself until you face the truth.*

Pearl Bailey

## Stress-Busting Strategy #1

# DETERMINE WHERE YOU STAND AND WHERE YOU WANT TO GO

*Do not weep;*
*do not wax indignant. Understand.*

BARUCH SPINOZA

**W**elcome to the world of low-stress money management. Of course, you may not be there yet. In fact, you may not know precisely how you're going to get there, or when. But the simple fact that you've picked up this book means that you're on your way to a better financial place, a place where you control your money, not vice versa.

This book addresses fourteen key concepts, and it contains an assortment of practical suggestions and timely tips. But at its core, the ideas in this text can be divided into two broad categories: planning and implementation. Planning, simply put, is determining where you are today, where you want to be tomorrow, and how you intend to get there. Implementation means putting your plan to work. Planning takes time—implementation takes discipline. It's as simple as that.

Whether you're reading a map or mapping out your financial future, it's important to know three things. First, you need to know your starting point. Second, you need to know your destination. Third, you must decide upon the route you intend to take. If you're reading a map, the beginning point is some-times made clear by a bright red "X" followed by the words, "You are here." From a financial perspective, your starting point begins with an accurate accounting of your monthly income and expenses.

At first glance, the job of figuring out your financial starting point—and putting it down on paper—may seem unnecessary. After all, you probably have an accurate idea of your monthly income (more likely than not, it's the number you see on your paycheck). And you should have, at the very least, a general idea of your expenses too. You're probably paying several of the same bills month after month, some of which you can recite by heart. For example, mortgage payment, rent, insurance, car payment. And you should also have a general idea of your other bills, including the ones that vary from month to month. So, if you have a general idea of your monthly income and expenses, why should you take the time to put these things down on paper? Because the simple act of writing down income and expenses provides a clear, unambiguous answer to a very important question: *Are you living at a profit, or not?*

To avoid financial stress and achieve financial peace, you must ultimately find a way to earn more money than you spend. Otherwise, you're sending Old Man Trouble a personal invitation to visit your house at a time of his choosing. You may not know precisely when Mr. Trouble will come knocking, but of this you can be sure: he's bound to show up sooner or later. Probably sooner.

Far too many people "never quite get around" to making a written budget. Oftentimes, these folks are afraid of the things that their budgets might reveal. They tell themselves that they're simply "too busy to budget" or that they're "bad with numbers." But perhaps there's a deeper, less obvious reason for their hesitation. Many of these folks possess a subconscious dread, an unspoken fear that their budgets may contain bad news. They're fearful that the cold, hard facts may simply be too cold and too hard to bear. This kind of thinking is misguided because, when it comes to managing money, ignorance isn't bliss. Never has been. Never will be.

So, if you've been putting off the job of formulating a written household budget, ask yourself why. And then, after that long pause while you struggle, unsuccessfully, for a logical answer, begin your journey toward financial security by taking the following steps:

**Step 1: Ask Yourself Where Things Stand Right Now.**
To get a clear sense of your financial situation, take time to gather information. It can be as simple as writing out a list of monthly income and monthly expenses, and then comparing the two. Don't get bogged down. If you don't know how much you're spending in an area, make an educated guess. Your goal is to find out if you spend more than you earn or earn more than you spend. Some important expense categories include:

- Housing: House payment or rent, homeowner's or renter's insurance, maintenance costs
- Utilities: Electricity, water, gas, trash, internet, cable

- Food: Groceries and dining out
- Transportation: Car payment, fuel, maintenance, auto insurance
- Clothing
- Child Care
- Insurance: Health, life, disability, long-term care
- Consumer Debt: Includes any other outstanding obligations
- Miscellaneous Expenses: Anticipate unexpected items that add up over time

Don't forget to include once-a-year expenses such as gifts for Christmas and birthdays.

Estimate the annual totals and divide by 12 to arrive at your average monthly expenses.

Then, to see where you stand, compare your monthly income to your monthly expenses.

**Step 2: Ask Yourself Where You'd Like to Go.** Jot down your most pressing financial goals. What changes would you like to make to reduce your financial stress? Some goals to consider might include:

- Paying off all credit cards
- Paying off other forms of consumer debt

- Saving funds for emergencies
- Setting aside money for vehicle repairs
- Buying a house instead of renting
- Setting aside money for a child's education
- Setting aside money for retirement

**Step 3: Ask Yourself What Steps You Need to Take.**
Map out some of the most important steps you can take on the journey from financial stress to financial security. Be specific as you make note of the things you can do to improve your situation. Some possible steps include the following:

- Consider ways to increase your income (a second job, a career change, or additional education, for example);
- Make a spending plan that balances income and expenses;
- Pay with cash to avoid amassing credit-card debt;
- Make more than minimum payments on credit cards;
- Start saving for future needs (perhaps a down-payment on a house, or tires for the car, or new appliances, for example).

We always suggest that you put your plans on paper and review them often. A written commitment to your goals will help you keep a positive attitude and push through obstacles as they arise.

*Let our advance worrying become advance thinking and planning.*

Winston Churchill

Winston Churchill's advice, which was given during the darker days of World War II, still applies to a wide range of activities, including matters of life and debt. Sometimes, when we're engulfed by financial concerns, we're tempted to worry, to complain, to stress out, and to do precious little else. Such behavior is counterproductive because, in the words of the iconic baseball executive Branch Rickey, "Worry is simply thinking the same thing over and over again and not doing anything about it." A better strategy, by far, is to worry less and do more. So, the challenge we all face is this: How do we stop worrying about—and start working to solve—the problems that are causing us distress? The answer, in most cases, isn't too complicated. We must simply take a deep breath and get started.

When it comes to solving problems, procrastination

is the enemy. So, we can't wait for the perfect moment to begin. And, we can't focus so intently on our fears that we lose sight of our objectives. Instead, we must begin attacking the problem, whatever it happens to be, even if we'd rather not. Sometimes, even a small beginning is enough to break the chains of procrastination and denial.

If, in the past, you've hesitated to attack your financial challenges head-on, today is a perfect day to cast off the chains of procrastination by figuring out where you stand financially and where you want to go. Once you've completed the three steps mentioned above, you'll have followed Churchill's advice by converting advance worry into advance thinking and planning. By doing so, you will have begun your journey toward financial peace and security. You'll have a better idea about the realities of your current situation, and you'll have a list of specific steps you can take to begin relieving financial stress. So what's next? Now, it's time to embark upon the second leg of your journey: compiling a written financial plan.

# A FEW MORE THOUGHTS
# ABOUT PLANNING

*Wisdom consists in the anticipation
of consequences.*

NORMAN COUSINS

*Plan your work. Without a system,
you'll feel swamped.*

NORMAN VINCENT PEALE

*It is better to have an ambitious
plan than none at all.*

WINSTON CHURCHILL

*The future belongs to those
who prepare for it.*

RALPH WALDO EMERSON

*I can give you a six-word formula for success:
Think things through and follow through.*

EDDIE RICKENBACKER

# 2

## THE QUESTION

I have a general idea of my monthly income and expenses, but I'm still feeling stressed. So what should I do next?

## THE ANSWER

Once you have a general idea of your monthly income and expenses, it's time to get specific with a detailed budget and a simple financial plan.

*Budgeting is telling your money where to go instead of asking it where it went.*

JOHN MAXWELL

**Stress-Busting Strategy #2**

# REDUCE STRESS WITH A WRITTEN BUDGET AND A FINANCIAL PLAN

*Good planning and hard work lead to prosperity, but hasty shortcuts lead to poverty.*
PROVERBS 21:5 NLT

In the previous chapter, you made general notes about the current state of your personal finances. Now it's time to get specific. It's time to start crafting a written budget and a simple financial plan.

A poll by the American Psychological Association showed money to be the most significant cause of stress among Americans. Over 75 percent of those polled ranked money above health problems, relationships, and family responsibilities as a significant source of anxiety. A majority of both men and women said they were unsatisfied with the current state of their finances. We weren't really surprised by these statistics. What *was* surprising, though, was this: the age-group most concerned about finances was not the over-65 crowd; the most concerned group was comprised of Millennials. The poll showed that a whopping 80 percent of Americans age 18-32 cited money as their biggest stressor.

In our self-help society, you'll find a near-endless stream of advice concerning ways to deal with financial anxiety. Much of the advice is good, but some of it is not. Recently a TV talk-show guest suggested the following four remedies for the money blues: Remedy #1: give a friend a mani ure; Remedy #2: meditate; Remedy #3 splurge on yourself; Remedy #4 learn to knit. As advice goes, we'd put that list in the "not good" category. Feel-good strategies like these may quiet your nerves temporarily, but they certainly don't address the real problem. Instead of splurging, knitting, manicuring, or meditating, you should try a different tactic: planning.

After years of working with people on their finances, we've learned that the biggest problem—the main source of financial anxiety—is uncertainty. Families stress out because they don't know where they are, where they're going, or how to change their situation.

Our advice to worried couples is simple, straightforward, and effective. We tell them that the smartest way to tackle money stress is to make a plan and then begin working that plan. The planning process shines a bright light on all the shadowy unknowns.

When you don't know where you stand on money matters, you'll be stressed by the many surprises that pop up. And, you'll subject your psyche to intermittent episodes of apprehension and dread whenever your thoughts turn to matters of money. But, once you've made a detailed analysis of your income and expenses, and once you've established a written plan that clearly demonstrates how you can make more money than you spend, you'll begin to feel better about yourself and your future. So, let the stress reducing begin. And, it begins with a budget.

### Step 1: Make a Budget and Stick to It.

If you're like most of us, calculating your income will be relatively easy to estimate. Simply take a look at your paystubs for the last few months and you'll probably have an accurate estimate of the money coming in. But estimating your expenses may take a little more time, especially if you haven't kept great records in the past. One way to tackle the problem is to think through a typical week of expenses—guess if you have to—and then multiply that number by 52 to achieve at a yearly estimate. Divide by 12 and you have your monthly figure. Remember that all you need is a snapshot. You won't achieve perfect accuracy—nobody does—but you'll have a better sense of your current financial standing.

## A FEW BUDGETING BASICS

- Your budget should be realistic. It should be based on the actual income and expenses, not pie-in-the-sky projections that you're unlikely to achieve.
- You should put your budget on paper, or if you're computer savvy, you may wish to use an electronic spreadsheet (Google Sheets offers free online budgeting templates).
- Your budget should include once-a-year expenses such as Christmas, birthdays, and vacations.
- If you're married, you should create your budget in cooperation with your spouse.
- You should leave room in your budget for surprises, and you should expect them.
- If your budget reflects more expenses than

income, you must find ways to cut your expenses, increase your income, or both.

- Once you have a written budget, you should review it regularly and compare it to actual results.

With those basics out of the way, here's a form you can use to help in the budgeting process:

## SAMPLE MONTHLY BUDGET

### Income:
Job #1: Salary / Commissions (after Withholding)
Job #2: Salary / Commissions (after Withholding)
Business or Interest Income
Other Income

Total Monthly Income

### Expenses
Rent
Mortgage Payment (Include Property Tax and Insurance)
Household Upkeep / Maintenance / Association Fees
Food (Groceries)

Food (Dining Out)

Automobile / Transportation (Car Payment, Gas, Insurance, Maintenance, etc.)

Out-of-Pocket Medical Expenses and Deductibles

Personal Insurance (Life, Health, Disability, etc.)

Utilities (Electricity, Water, Gas, Land Line)

Mobile Phone and Data Plan

Educational Expenses (Books, Tuition, etc.)

Debt Payments / Credit Card Debt

Travel (Includes Annual Vacations)

Gifts

Seasonal Expenses (Christmas, Birthdays, etc.)

Additional Income Tax (Over and Above Withholding)

Internet Service

Charitable Giving

Other Expenses / Unexpected Expenses

Total Monthly Expenses

**Income Minus Expenses (Excess Cash Flow)**

## Step 2: Make Short-Term Plans for the Money You Save.

Have you ever gotten lost in an unfamiliar city? Not knowing where you are or where you're going can be a frightening experience. And so it is with money. If you're not sure where you are financially or where you intend to go you'll be anxious or stressed or both. The solution, of course, is to create a clear financial roadmap that tells you where you are today and where you plan to be tomorrow. Once you've decided where you're going, your fear melts away and you begin to feel encouraged. So after you've formulated a budget, the next step is to start setting goals for your money.

Look ahead and ask yourself about the changes you will make to reduce your financial stress. Would you like to create an emergency fund? Do you want to save for a car or for a down-payment on a house? Should you pay off those high-interest credit cards? Or open a savings account for future needs? Each of these steps brings you closer to your financial goals and the stress-relieving sense that you've got things under control. Write down these goals and set a deadline. What can you accomplish in three months? Which goals can you achieve in a year?

So, what do you do after you've established these exciting goals? This is where many families have trouble. Enthusiasm gives way to inertia. And pessimism. And discouragement. And procrastination.

When people become stuck, we advise them to think about short-term goals and the steps that are necessary to achieve those goals. Once they figure out their next step, they inevitably regain energy and momentum. Therefore, your next task is to chart the course that will take from where you are (now) to the place you want to be (in 12 to 24 months). The planning process takes time, but it's time well spent. As you create smart, realistic goals, you'll decide where you'd like to go in the next few months, and you'll determine exactly how you're going to get there.

Below is an example of a person who, through careful budgeting, can save $500 per month. Here's an example of the short-term goals that person can accomplish in just 24 short months:

# AN EXAMPLE OF SHORT-TERM GOAL-SETTING

Reaching My Financial Goals in __24__ Months

**Amount I can save each month: $500**

| Goal | Amount Required to Accomplish Goal | Amount I Can Pay Each Month | Time Required to Accomplish Goal |
|------|------------------------------------|-----------------------------|----------------------------------|
| Put $1,000 in an emergency fund | $1,000 | $500 | 2 months |
| Pay off $3,000 in credit-card debt | $3,000 | $500 | 6 months |
| Put $2,000 into a retirement account | $2,000 | $500 | 4 Months |
| Put $3,000 into a savings account | $3,000 | $500 | 6 Months |
| Put $3,000 into a mutual fund | $3,000 | $500 | 6 Months |

In the above example, it's easy to see how much progress a person can make in two years if he or she establishes a budget, sticks to it, and saves $500 each month. Perhaps you can't save that much right now. That's okay. What you can do is this: you can formulate a budget that allows you to make more money than you spend each month. It may be hard; it may be challenging; it may require sacrifices; but you can do it. When you do, you can set short-term financial goals that make sense. And you're on your way.

## Step 3: Establish a Few Specific Long-Term Goals and Make Plans to Accomplish Them.

Now comes the fun part: setting long-term goals and making long-term plans. Why do we call it fun? Because your long-term goals and the plans you make to achieve those goals will demonstrate, on paper, the amazing things you can accomplish when you expand your time-horizon to years instead of months.

Unless you're independently wealthy (in which case you're probably not reading this book) or unless you've just won the lottery (FYI: We don't recommend playing the lottery because gambling, in any form, can be dangerous to your financial health), you should not expect to achieve long-term financial security in 12 months, in 24 months, or, for that matter, in 60 months. For most of us, achieving *real* financial security takes years. So, if you're looking for a short-term fix to a long-term problem, you'll probably be disappointed. But before you become discouraged and close this book, consider this: the simple act of setting realistic long-term goals will help you reduce stress by demonstrating, once and for all, that you can perform near-miraculous financial feats if you have enough discipline and have enough time.

For example, consider the effort that's required to purchase a house and to pay for it. First, you must find the house, apply for a mortgage, and make a down payment. Then you must close on the house, you must move in, and you must begin making mortgage payments each month. You must also spend money for utilities and taxes and maintenance and insurance. These costs undoubtedly take a substantial chunk out of your paycheck, but you understand that you're not just keeping a roof over your head; you're also building a financial nest egg in the form of home equity. (BTW: The term "equity" refers to the difference between the value of your house and the remaining balance on the mortgage.)

As your house appreciates (as it probably will), your equity gradually goes up too. And, unless you've taken out an interest-only loan (which we don't advise), you will also be paying down the outstanding balance on your loan. Paying off a home loan is a gradual process that usually takes between 15 and 30 years. It's a worthy long-term goal that requires long-term thinking and plenty of discipline. But it's possible. Plenty of people do it, and if you have sufficient discipline and sufficient time, you can do it too.

We know what you may be thinking right now. You may be saying to yourself, "I'll never own my home 'free and clear.' It's impossible." But if that's what you're thinking, we ask you to reconsider the word "impossible." Time and again we hear stories about individuals who earned modest incomes but somehow managed to make millions. One such person was Ronald Reed.

Mr. Reed, who was a lifelong resident of Brattleboro, Vermont, came from humble beginnings. He was the first person in his family to graduate from high school and, after serving in World War II, he found work as a gas station attendant and as a janitor at J. C. Penny's department store. Reed was a married man with two children, so he had expenses. But he watched his money carefully, he saved money from every paycheck, and he bought stocks. Mr. Reed wasn't a day-trader and he wasn't a gambler; he invested in well-known companies and held onto those blue-chip stocks for years. Using this simple save-and-invest strategy, Mr. Reed proved, once and for all, that you don't have to earn a huge salary to amass millions.

When he died at age 92, Ronald Reed had accumulated an estate of $8 million dollars, $6 million of which he left to the local library and hospital. Reed's stepson said, "He was a hard worker, but I don't think anybody had an idea that he was a multimillionaire." *The Wall Street Journal* reported that Mr. Reed "owned at least 95 stocks at the time of his death, many of which he had held for years, if not decades."

Ronald Reed's story reminds us that the old-fashioned principles of "earn, save, buy, and hold" can still work financial miracles for people who live frugally, save consistently, invest sensibly, and keep reinvesting their earnings. So if you're thinking that you'll never escape the financial quicksand of debt—or that you can never pay off your home mortgage—think again. If a married janitor with two kids living in small-town Vermont can work financial miracles, you can too.

Ronald Reed had long-term financial goals. So what are yours? To help clarify your thoughts, take time to write down one or two long-term financial goals and the steps you'll need to take to achieve them. Here's an example of the long-term goal we discussed above: buying a home and paying off a home mortgage.

# LONG-TERM FINANCIAL GOAL:

## Example #1: Buying a Home and Paying Off the Mortgage

| My Long-Term Goal: | Own my home and pay off the mortgage before I retire. |
|---|---|
| **Steps Required to Achieve My Goal** | **Estimated Time Required to Achieve My Goal** |
| Step 1: Save enough money for a substantial down payment | 3 years |
| Step 2: Purchase 1st home with 25-year mortgage and build equity for 5 years. | 5 years |
| Step 3: Sell 1st home and use the equity to make a bigger down payment on 2nd home. Take out a 15-year mortgage and stay put until the mortgage is paid off. | 15 years |
| Total Time Required to Achieve Goal | 23 years |

# AND HERE'S ANOTHER EXAMPLE
# OF A WORTHY LONG-TERM FINANCIAL GOAL:

## Example #2: Saving $100,000 in a Retirement Account

| My Long-Term Goal: | To have $100,000 in my retirement account |
|---|---|
| **Scenarios That Can Achieve My Goal** | **Time Required to Reach My Goal** |
| Scenario #1: Save $250 a month; investments in the retirement account earn an average of 5% per year. | 19 years and 8 months |
| Scenario #2: Save $300 a month; investments in the retirement account earn an average of 6% per year. | 16 years and 5 months |
| Scenario #3: Save $400 a month; investments in the retirement account earn an average of 6% per year. | 13 years and 7 months |
| Scenario #4: Save $500 a month; investments in the retirement account earn an average of 7% per year. | 11 years and 7 months |

As you can easily see from the above examples, the bigger the goal, the longer its time horizon. Accumulating a six-figure retirement account can take a decade or more; paying off a home loan may take even longer than that. That's why it is imperative to begin charting your financial future as soon as possible. If you haven't already begun, today's a perfect day to start.

*Industry, perseverance,*
*and frugality make fortune yield.*

BEN FRANKLIN

—ᴍ—

## YOUR BUDGET + YOUR SHORT-TERM GOALS + YOUR LONG-TERM PLANS = YOUR FINANCIAL PLAN

**Creating a simple, straightforward financial plan can be accomplished in three steps:**

- First, you prepare—and adhere to—a budget that allows you to live at a profit.

- Next, you establish a series of attainable short-term goals.
- Finally, you formulate two or three long-term goals that will provide you and your family financial security in the years to come.

Will you summon the courage to make noble plans, and will you encourage you loved ones to do likewise? Hopefully, you'll answer with a resounding "Yes," and "Yes."

We believe that God has a plan for your life, an important plan, a plan that only you and He, working together, can fulfill. But there's a catch: you live in a world that entices you to waste your money, your resources, your energy, and your time. These temptations are impediments along your path, and they should be avoided whenever and wherever possible.

To focus on the financial strategies that will deliver you from stress and strain—and to minimize the time-wasting trivialities that threaten to drain your bank account—we encourage you make a sensible budget, to set achievable short-term goals, to formulate a few long-term goals, and to get busy turning those goals into reality. Don't settle for second-best, and don't sell yourself short. Even if your goals seem to stretch you to the limit, don't be discouraged. No goal is too big and no plan is too ambitious for you and God—working together—to accomplish.

*"For I know the plans I have for you,"
declares the L*ORD*, "plans to prosper you
and not to harm you, plans to give
you hope and a future. Then you
will call upon me and come and pray
to me, and I will listen to you."*

J*EREMIAH* 29:11–12 NIV

## A FEW THOUGHTS ABOUT GOALS AND GOAL SETTING

*Success is the progressive
realization of a worthy goal.*

E*ARL* N*IGHTINGALE*

*A good goal is like a strenuous exercise—
it makes you stretch.*

M*ARY* K*AY* A*SH*

*Life's up and downs provide windows
of opportunity to determine your values
and goals. Think of using all obstacles as
stepping stones to build the life you want.*

MARSHA SINETAR

*If you don't know where you are going,
you will probably end up somewhere else.*

LAURENCE J. PETER

*Ask yourself, "Where will I be 10 years
from now if I keep doing what I'm doing?"*

W. CLEMENT STONE

*A person has to have goals
for a day and for a lifetime.*

TED WILLIAMS

*My child, don't lose sight of
common sense and discernment.
Hang on to them,
for they will refresh your soul.
They are like jewels on a necklace.*

PROVERBS 3:21–22 NLT

# 3

## THE QUESTION

It seems like I'm making the same
money mistakes over and over again.
Why is it taking me so long to learn lessons
that I should have learned long ago?

## THE ANSWER

Whether you realize it or not, you have a
"money personality," a way of interacting with
your world, your friends, your family, and your
checkbook. To gain a better understanding
of your spending habits—and to gain better
control over your finances—you should take
a careful look at your own personality style.

*Every man ought to try to know
all he can about himself.*

C. H. SPURGEON

*No one is truly literate who
cannot read his own heart.*

ERIC HOFFER

**Stress-Busting Strategy #3**

# UNDERSTAND YOUR OWN MONEY PERSONALITY

*I think, somehow, we learn who we*
*really are and live with that decision.*

ELEANOR ROOSEVELT

**D**ad, do you know what kind of animal you are? Are you a lion, an otter, a golden retriever, or a beaver?"

This unexpected question came from our daughter after school one day several years ago. Her class had been exploring their unique personality types and had taken a test to discover which of those four animals best matched their behavioral style. For her, the test had revealed that she was a beaver-lion. So what did that mean?

The test she'd taken was a version of the DISC,

a popular assessment that groups people into four categories of personality traits. Authors Gary Smalley and John Trent used animals to make the test easy to understand for children. Here's how it works: D is for Dominant or Driver; this was the lion part of our daughter's result indicating her bent toward leadership. The letter I is for Inspiring or Influencing, represented by the fun-loving otter. S stands for Steady or Stable, symbolized by the relaxed and reliable golden retriever. C is for Correct or Compliant, signified by our child's other animal label, the precise and industrious beaver.

Our family has enjoyed using these descriptive terms as a way to gain a better understanding of ourselves. We've got lions, beavers and a bit of golden retriever at our house, but nobody is 100 percent otter. Which "animals" live in your home? Is one of you assertive, focused, and interested in the bottom line? She may be a lion—forceful, strong-willed, and direct. Maybe a member of your family is a great communicator: optimistic, talkative, and friendly to everyone he meets. He's probably an otter. The golden retriever in your group is known for being patient, practical, even-keeled and a good listener. If one of you really enjoys gathering facts and details, is thorough in all activities, and tends toward being analytical—that's the beaver.

Each of us has a "money personality" that influences how we think about money and how we manage our financial resources. So what's your money personality? And what about your spouse? The better you understand yourself and your loved ones, the better you'll handle the inevitable money skirmishes that may crop up from time to time.

Each of the four DISC personality types tackles financial decisions differently. For example, when thinking about a car purchase, the decisive lion tends to make a decision quickly after gathering the most pertinent information. Lions want to get it done; they aren't as interested in doing the detailed research and the price comparisons that a beaver would think necessary. When choosing what style of car to buy, otters tend to think about fun and flash while golden retrievers focus on practicality and comfort. With differing styles and perspectives, there's always the possibility of a conflict. On the other hand, as different personalities bring their strengths to the conversation, everybody can contribute to a better decision.

The discipline of saving is another area in which people typically do things their own way. Some personalities are more apt to save their money while others are more likely to spend. For a beaver, a systematic savings plan is preferred because beavers don't want to be caught off guard. Beavers feel good when they have an emergency fund that will provide a safe financial haven should disaster may come their way. Lions are often good savers as well, especially when the savings plan is connected to a desirable goal they can achieve. In contrast, live-in-the-moment otters and easy-going golden retrievers aren't as motivated to save for a rainy day.

Charitable giving is handled differently among the various money personalities. Golden Retrievers and Otters, the more relationship-oriented types, often give generously and spontaneously as they become aware of needs; they're quick to give, even if they can't really afford it. It's a decision of the heart. Lions and Beavers, the more task-focused types, would rather decide on giving ahead of time and write a check for the same affordable amount every month. For them, the decision is less likely to be affected by emotions.

Tax season highlights big differences in money personalities. Beavers are meticulous at record keeping; some even enjoy doing taxes without professional assistance. They tend to be conservative with deductions and take care to follow the rules. And, they don't like to get refunds; it means they made an error and overestimated their withholdings. Lions may hire a tax preparer to save time, but if they do their own taxes, they're more aggressive with deductions and willing to take risks in order "to win." They dislike refunds, too, because it means they've lost income as the government held their money at no interest. Some golden retrievers may patiently wade through the self-preparation of tax forms, but they may put it off as long as possible. If they get a refund, part of it might be put to practical use to pay bills. Otters would definitely prefer to have someone else handle all the details of tax preparation. Their fun-loving social streak might tempt them to spend a tax refund on an enjoyable experience with family or friends.

In these few examples, it's obvious that each personality style has a particular approach to problem solving. The styles are not necessarily right or wrong; they're just different. For couples, the differences often complement each other and make life better for both. For example, an otter married to a beaver might sound like trouble, but their partnership can produce surprising results. For example, in preparation for their summer vacation, the beaver may be willing to invest time and energy in planning and working out all the details of a fabulous trip. That's a service to the otter, for whom details are a drag. While on the vacation, the otter's optimism and excitement may serve to intensify the fun and magnify the enjoyment for the beaver.

Learning to respect the differences and to recognize the value of each style will not only lead to more harmonious relationships but also to a well-rounded and effective response to the financial challenges we all face. Vive la différence!

---

## A FEW MORE THOUGHTS ABOUT SELF-KNOWLEDGE

*The longest journey is the journey inward.*

DAG HAMMARSKJÖLD

*Observe all men, thyself most.*

BEN FRANKLIN

*Learn to be what you are, and learn to resign with a good grace all that you are not.*

HENRI FRÉDÉRIC AMIEL

*Sometimes it is more important
to discover what one cannot do
than what one can do.*

LIN YU-T'ANG

*Never try to be an expert
if you are not. Build on your strengths
and find strong people
to do the other necessary tasks.*

PETER DRUCKER

*The delights of self-discovery
are always available.*

GAIL SHEEHY

*The wise people will shine like
the brightness of the sky.
Those who teach others to live right
will shine like stars forever and ever.*

DANIEL 12:3 NCV

# 4

## THE QUESTION

I want to get serious about managing money, but I'm not sure if my family is ready to go along with the plan. What should I do?

## THE ANSWER

You should sit down and have a family meeting to inform everyone of your intentions. And, just as importantly, you should enlist their support. Otherwise, you'll probably experience pushback, conflict, and power struggles over money.

*A family splintered by feuding will fall apart*

MARK 3:25 NLT

**Stress-Busting Strategy #4**

# MAKE MONEY MANAGEMENT A FAMILY AFFAIR

*A family is a place where principles
are hammered and honed
on the anvil of everyday living.*

CHARLES SWINDOLL

Managing money wisely can be—and should be—a family affair. It's important for couples to manage their money cooperatively, and it's just as important for parents to pass on money-management skills to their kids.

Have you and your family members talked openly about the way you manage money? And, just as importantly, have you all learned the subtle art of cooperation? If so, you have learned the wisdom of "give and take," not the foolishness of "me first."

Cooperation is the art of compromising on many little things while keeping your eyes on one big thing: your family's future. The happiest families live within their means. And, the happiest families work together as a team. So, if you want to build a strong financial future, make sure your family is aware of your money-management style, your plans, and your values. Make money management a team effort, a working partnership between you, your family, and your Creator. It's the best way to manage your money and your life.

## MONEY AND MARRIAGE: KEEP TALKING!

We chuckled as we left the doctor's office on that fateful day in 1991. We were engaged and had gone to the tiny clinic to get the blood tests we needed before we could apply for a marriage license in Pennsylvania, where we were to be married. Because the test wasn't required in Virginia, where we both lived at the time, we traveled to a community health clinic across the border in West Virginia. And when our blood tests were completed, we left giggling because we'd just experienced what must have been the shortest premarital counseling session in history.

The elderly doctor spoke to us for about 15 seconds, his voice a resigned monotone as he scribbled notes and signed documents. "Marriage is hard work," he sighed. "Keep talking. That's my advice. Keep talking."

We nodded and thanked him, trying our best to hide our amusement at his emotionless delivery and perfunctory advice.

Although it may have seemed irrelevant to us at that moment, we've recounted the doctor's short speech many times. He was right about marriage. It takes serious effort. And, his advice to "keep talking," which sounded simplistic at the time, was perhaps the best marital counseling we've ever received. Through a myriad of challenges, our ability to communicate with each other has been the key to a healthy, growing relationship.

Talking to each other has been especially important in the area of finances. Larry Burkett, a noted financial author, said that "money is either the best or the worst area of communication in our marriages." To remain on course financially and relationally, we've learned how to talk about money and how to listen too. Here are some of the communication lessons we've learned:

## CARVE OUT TIME TO TALK

Meaningful communication about money doesn't seem to happen for us unless we schedule it. We might try to talk about a spending decision while we're running around doing other errands, but too often we end up frustrated because we're guessing at account balances or struggling to remember the amount of a bill.

To make financial discussions worthwhile, we usually need to set a specific time; we need to have some figures in front of us; and, we need access to our computer, a calculator, a calendar, paper, and a pencil. With those resources at hand, we can discuss our current financial status, review upcoming expenses, monitor our spending plan, and set goals for savings or investments. Some money gurus call this planned conversation a "business meeting." Although that term doesn't sound very romantic, a meeting like this can improve a marriage. It's a chance to look at the facts, to discuss feelings, to plan, and to pray together.

## MAKE IT ROUTINE

Sitting down at least once a month to talk things over helps in a number of ways. For one thing, the "meetings" can be shorter. A twenty- to thirty-minute financial review fits more comfortably into our evening schedule than a two-hour slog through months of bills and statements. Brief meetings tend to end on a cheerier note as well, since neither of us has been overwhelmed by too many details.

Another advantage of regular financial discussions is that we're more unified in our approach to the challenges that arise. We believe that the unity comes from the mutual support that we give each other by sharing, by listening, and by helping each other think through financial decisions.

## TELL ALL

In our financial coaching, we've worked with couples whose money woes have wrenched them apart and taken them to the brink of divorce. In many cases, the problem that fractured the marriage was a lack of honesty.

When one partner is covering up spending or

debt—or hiding income or savings—it's only a matter of time before the other partner discovers the deception. In one case, a couple was sitting with a loan officer reviewing documents when the husband noticed some unfamiliar credit cards on their credit report. It wasn't identity theft; it was debt that his wife had hidden from him. The arguing couple left in embarrassment without completing the loan. It was a sad scene.

Think, for a moment, how the wife must have felt when her secretive credit card accounts were discovered. And, think how the husband must have reacted to this act of money-management betrayal. This example proves, yet again, that deception doesn't work for long. As Jesus proclaimed in Luke 12:2–3 (NLT):

> *Everything that is covered up will be revealed, and all that is secret will be made known to all. Whatever you have said in the dark will be heard in the light, and what you have whispered behind closed doors will be shouted from the housetops for all to hear!*

Dishonesty is toxic to a marriage. When the truth comes out—as eventually it must—trust is damaged and the marriage suffers immensely. For this reason, we advocate full disclosure of every dollar earned, spent, borrowed, or saved. That kind of sharing requires intentional communication as well as grace and understanding.

We don't advocate splitting the bills or using separate checking accounts to pay bills. Instead, we encourage couples to work together, to respect their differences, to negotiate, and to compromise. Both partners should have a little cash to spend as they see fit, but decisions about bigger purchases should be made jointly. The resulting conversations provide opportunities to understand each other's desires, to hear one another's concerns, and to work creatively together.

## DREAM TOGETHER

Talking about money can be tedious at times. To keep things exciting, couples should talk together and imagine together about the future. They should talk about financial success: what it will look like and what it will feel like. For some couples, success is freedom from debt; for others, it's the ability to give generously. Others may plan for the day when one parent can be home full-time with the kids. And, many couples dream of a comfortable retirement. Discussing goals such as these can enliven discussions, spark creativity, and motivate a spirit of partnership.

Throughout our marriage, we've spent many hours talking about our financial hopes and dreams. These conversations haven't centered on investment portfolios or account balances. Instead, we've discussed the places we'd like to live, the vacations we'd like to take, and the ways we can make life better for our children. We've talked about dream jobs and dream houses. We've spent happy hours sharing our plans and hopes, but in the final analysis, those discussions were less about money and more about our relationship—our choice to live our lives together and to share everything. Along the way, we've grown much closer, and we've cheered each other on toward our goals.

## KEEP TALKING!

As that crusty, old doctor told us, marriage is hard work. And, dealing with money matters can be challenging too. So, married couples should make the commitment to review finances regularly, to share responsibility, to be honest with each other, and to stay positive. And above all, couples should keep talking. That's our advice: Keep talking!

—⟋⟍—

# A FEW MORE THOUGHTS ABOUT MARRIAGE AND COOPERATION

*There is no more lovely,*
*friendly or charming relationship,*
*communion or company,*
*than a good marriage.*

MARTIN LUTHER

*Your spouse is your closest relative*
*and is entitled to depend on you*
*as a common ally, supporter,*
*and champion.*

AARON BECK

*Marriage is a partnership*
*in which individual selfishness has*
*to be surrendered for mutual gain.*

NORMAN VINCENT PEALE

*Each partner should take
full responsibility
for improving the relationship.*

AARON BECK

*Cooperation is a two-way street, but for
too many couples, it's the road less traveled.*

MARIE T. FREEMAN

*A successful marriage is not a gift;
it is an achievement.*

ANN LANDERS

*Success in marriage is more than finding
the right person; it is being the right person.*

ROBERT BROWNING

# WORDS OF FINANCIAL WISDOM
# FOR OUR CHILDREN

*Train up a child in the way he should go,
and when he is old he will not depart from it.*

PROVERBS 22:6 NKJV

A friend of ours can still remember the feeling of desolation that washed over him when, as a child, he saw his prized possession—a two-wheeled bike—mashed into a pretzel under the tires of his neighbor's van. Our friend had laid the small bicycle down on the driveway behind the passenger's side of the van before joining the gaggle of kids playing on the lawn. Just a few minutes later, they all heard the screeching crunch. The neighbor, although relieved that it was only a bike that he'd hit, spoke harshly: "I'm sorry about your bike, but this is what happens when you don't take care of your stuff."

It was a memorable life lesson: "Take care of your stuff."

Like many life-altering bits of wisdom, this lesson was learned the hard way. As parents, we recognize that tough experiences are sometimes the best teachers. Even so, we try to offer our children less painful lessons if we can. On the subject of money, we have opportunities in each season of childhood to distill our advice into a proverbial truth—a simple lesson in financial reality that can help our kids grow in wisdom. Here are our age-appropriate favorites from preschool through high school:

## THE BIG LESSON FOR KIDS UNDER AGE SIX: TAKE CARE OF YOUR STUFF

Most of us can recall a few, sad stories like the one our friend shared about his crushed bicycle. These tales can be powerful teaching tools for young children. The reality comes in two parts. First, the kids understand that toys and other possessions can get lost, broken, or taken. Second, they recognize that they can avoid those painful losses by paying attention to and by caring for the things they own. This may mean picking up and putting away toys, bringing bikes or scooters in when it's raining, or making sure the cat doesn't shred the Barbie clothes.

Here is one Biblical proverb that reinforces this lesson: "You should take good care of your sheep and goats, because wealth and honor don't last forever" Proverbs 27:23–24 (CEV).

## THE BIG LESSON FOR KIDS AGES SIX TO TEN: IT TAKES MONEY TO ACQUIRE STUFF

When you were a child, did you ever trudge alongside your mom or dad, walking up and down aisle after endless aisle at the grocery store? If so, that was probably one of your earliest exposures to the value of money.

It was in the grocery store that we taught our own kids what it means to be savvy shoppers. We took our time to compare prices in search of the best deals. Sometimes, for the sake of a bargain, we'd even stop at more than one store per trip. Groan. Of course our kids would have preferred to be playing in the back yard, but those grocery-store marathons were teachable moments.

Children in the six-to-ten age group are capable of fetching the canned tomato sauce, examining the unit prices on the mounted price tags, and choosing the best value for the money. Before the age of debit cards, parents who paid in cash could demonstrate the cost of a cartful of food with a handful of bills. Now that we pay in plastic, it requires a bit more explanation. Either way it's time well spent.

Ken knows another way for your child to learn

that stuff costs money, but he doesn't recommend it. When he was in first grade, he pilfered a pack of candy while waiting with the family in the checkout line. When his mom discovered his transgression, she drove Ken back to the store for a short confessional with the manager. The man smiled and offered forgiveness as he took Ken's nickel.

The idea here is to help kids connect value with currency. In the Bible, the virtuous wife "considers a field and buys it" (Proverbs 31:16 NIV). It's the ability to "consider"—to weigh, to compare, and to choose—that indicates growing financial wisdom.

## THE BIG LESSON FOR KIDS AGES ELEVEN TO THIRTEEN: TO EARN MONEY, YOU NEED TO WORK

Something happens in the "tween" years that makes this group very attractive to advertisers. Tweens become self-directed consumers. By one estimate, kids in this age group spend $30 billion of their own money each year and influence another $150 billion of their parents' spending!

As our two children passed through this stage,

they were drawn to different kinds of purchases: computer games for him and iTunes downloads for her. They had two options for earning the money needed: to earn commissions from us or to operate a business of their own. In either case, we insisted that they actually worked for their money.

We learned about the "commissions" concept from Dave Ramsey. It differs from an allowance; instead of paying our children for breathing, we exchange money for their services. For example, Margaret earned cash by removing and washing all of the window screens at our house. This "commissioned" work was in addition to the many daily and weekly chores our kids were—and still are—asked to do just because they're part of the team.

The other way to earn money is to own and operate a business of some kind: to make something, to raise something, or to do some service and get paid for it. The son of a family friend has been mowing lawns for years. After investing some of his earnings in a riding mower, the boy was able to mow more lawns in less time and earn more money for the car he wanted. Similarly, our children have each raised laying hens and sold the eggs for a profit. One thing they've learned from the stinky, messy work of caring for hens: sometimes you'll love your work and sometimes you'll despise it, but if you do it well, you'll be rewarded.

We use a Bible verse as a reminder that nobody ever earned a dollar by just gabbing about it. The verse is Proverbs 14:23 (NIV), which says "All hard work brings a profit, but mere talk leads only to poverty."

## THE BIG LESSON FOR KIDS AGES FOURTEEN TO EIGHTEEN: THINK AHEAD BY SAVING AND MAKING A BUDGET

When our son was sixteen and wanted a driver's license, he took the initiative not only to complete his "behind the wheel" training course but also to pay for it himself. Several months earlier, looking ahead to the cash flow we expected in our family budget, we let David know that he might need to wait a bit before we'd be able to fork over the fee for his driving course. Unwilling to endure a delay, our son saved the money and paid the tuition himself. Our expression of thanks was genuine; he truly helped us out. By thinking ahead, he was ready when the financial need arose.

Neither of our children has yet begun a serious

budget or a spending plan to support themselves. Even so, we've counseled so many couples over the years that we believe we'll know how to help. We'll first encourage them to track their income and their spending for a while. Next, we'll encourage them to track where their money is going and decide where they need to cut back. They'll probably be dreaming of some big purchases in the future, so we'll help them set a savings goal. To reach their goal more quickly, they may choose to earn more money or spend less. We'll talk about discerning between needs and wants, keeping their emotions in check, and avoiding comparisons with other kids their age. And we'll cheer them on as they learn the wisdom of having a plan of action.

Along the way, we may remind them of the wise counsel found in Proverbs 21:5 (NIV): "The plans of the diligent lead to profit as surely as haste leads to poverty."

Throughout every season and stage of our children's lives, we've done our best to teach our children age-appropriate lessons about managing money. We suggest you do likewise. And what's the best way to teach your kids about the peace and contentment that results from handling money wisely and well? By example, of course.

# A FEW MORE THOUGHTS ABOUT RAISING AND TEACHING OUR KIDS

*Each day of our lives
we make deposits in the
memory banks of our children.*

CHARLES SWINDOLL

*Children want their parents
more than they want
the junk we buy them.*

JAMES DOBSON

*To teach is to learn twice.*

JOSEPH JOUBERT

*The object of teaching a child
is to enable him to get along
without his teacher.*

ELBERT HUBBARD

*Children are not casual guests
in our homes. They have been
loaned to us temporarily
for the purpose of loving them
and instilling the values upon
which their lives will be built.*

JAMES DOBSON

*Children have more need
of models than critics.*

JOSEPH JOUBERT

*To teach is to learn twice.*

JOSEPH JOUBERT

*If you want to teach,
be a role model.
That's the most powerful
form of teaching.*

JOHN WOODEN

# 5

## THE QUESTION

I've been stressed out about money
for a long time, and I know I need
to make changes, but I keep putting it off.
Why do I keep procrastinating?

## THE ANSWER

There can be many reasons
for your procrastination, but there's
only one solution: to get started.
Now. Whether you feel like it or not.

*God specializes in giving people a fresh start.*

RICK WARREN

*When you make a promise to God,*
*don't delay in following through,*
*for God takes no pleasure in fools.*
*Keep all the promises you make to him.*

ECCLESIASTES 5:4 NLT

## Stress-Busting Strategy #5

# GET STARTED NOW

*Do noble things,*
*do not dream them all day long.*

CHARLES KINGSLEY

When we're stressed, it's easy to put things off. Instead of doing the work that needs to be done today, we're tempted to flop down on the couch, to reach for the clicker, and to binge-watch. We tell ourselves that we'll "get around to it" tomorrow or next week or next month. But when tomorrow comes, we feel even more discouraged because we know that the task we're dreading today is the very same task we should have done yesterday or last week or last month.

The singer Joan Baez once advised that, "Action is the antidote to despair." And so it is with money management. The best antidote to money-stress is action. As

Antoine de Saint-Exupéry famously observed, "The time for action is now. It's never too late to do something."

The sooner you formulate a reasonable financial strategy—and the sooner you begin implementing your plan—the better. Today is better than tomorrow. Yesterday is better than today.

Life happens one day at a time, and that's precisely how we should tackle the challenges of managing our money. We should ask ourselves, "What can I do about it today?" And we should pray for the strength to do the things that need doing right now, in the present tense, utilizing the only moment that is readily available to us: this moment.

It's good to make plans for the future, of course. But planning is never enough. Once we've established our plans, the time to act upon them is now. The tougher the task, the sooner we should begin.

## DON'T BE AFRAID OF FAILURE

Tomorrow. It's a word that rolls easily off the tongue; perhaps too easily for most of us, especially when we're tempted to procrastinate. We tell ourselves that we'll get around to life's unpleasant tasks tomorrow or next week or soon. But all too often, tomorrow becomes never.

Sometimes, the reason for our hesitation is clear: we're afraid to fail. We focus too intently on the negative consequences of missing the mark, and we lose sight of the rich rewards that might be ours if we would only get started.

The author Dorthea Brande gave us a powerful antidote to procrastination. She wrote,

*All that is necessary to break the spell of inertia and frustration is this: Act as if it were impossible to fail. That is the talisman, the formula, the command of right-about-face which turns us from failure towards success.*

Maybe you've been hesitant to go "all in" with your financial plan. Maybe you've convinced yourself (wrongly) that you won't ever achieve your goals. Maybe you're plagued by self-doubt, or perhaps you're still haunted by mistakes of the past. If so, today—this very moment—is the appropriate time to cast off the chains of procrastination. Today is the day to begin.

*We have to start teaching ourselves not to be afraid.*

WILLIAM FAULKNER

## START SAVING AUTOMATICALLY FOR RETIREMENT: OUT OF SIGHT, OUT OF MIND

When we talk to families about the state of their financial health, there's a word that too many folks seem anxious to ignore. That word is "retirement." Far too many people are in denial about the fact that they will, in all probability, live long enough to out-live their meager savings. In fact, some people admit to us that when the retirement day arrives—if it ever does—they'll be content to live on whatever income they can pull together at the time.

In 2016, the Economic Policy Institute (EPI) conducted a study and found that half the families in America had less than $5,000 in retirement savings. And in 2018, another survey, conducted by Northwestern Mutual, found that over 20 percent of our fellow citizens have *nothing* saved for their golden years. Zero. Nada. Zilch. So how do these people plan to live out their final years? The answer, unfortunately, is Social Security.

Social Security was never intended to be the only source of a retiree income; it was designed to supplement retirement income. But far too many of our friends and neighbors are depending upon their government checks to make ends meet.

You should not—indeed must not—view Social Security as your only source of retirement income. In 2018, the average Social Security check was $1,404. That's $16,848 per year. To put that number in perspective, it's about $30 a month more than the poverty level for a 2-person household (as calculated by the Department of Health and Human Services). So, unless you intend to retire on poverty wages, with no room for error and no financial cushion for unexpected expenses, you need to start saving for retirement. Now.

The easiest way to save for retirement is to do it automatically: by automatic withdrawal from your paycheck or your bank account. When retirement savings are taken automatically from your pay, the whole process seems less painful. And that's good because saving for retirement is an essential element of your financial plan.

—⁓—

## KEN'S EXPERIENCE WITH RETIREMENT PLANNING: USE AUTOMATIC PAYMENTS

*After years of investing in my employer's 401(k) plan for retirement, I made a career change. Since the new* job's retirement benefits didn't start until I'd been employed for a full year, I thought it would be wise to open an IRA and continue my retirement savings plan, funding it on my own for that year.

Well, I'm sad to admit that six months after I started the new job, I still hadn't begun saving. Not a dollar. Yes, I'd emailed a trusted financial advisor for advice. And I had every intention of getting things rolling. But, like so many of the people I'd counseled over the years, I simply "hadn't gotten around" to opening up a new IRA. I was motivated, and I didn't want to lose momentum, but I was also busy with my new job. So I procrastinated. And then I did the calculations.

Where I had been working before, I saved 8 percent of my earnings and the employer kindly matched that, dollar for dollar. Therefore, to maintain the flow of money saved, I would simply need to deposit 16 percent of my gross pay into an IRA invested in mutual funds. Easy, right? It's more than I had been saving before, but we could certainly deal with it for a year. Unfortunately, when it came time to get started, I froze psychologically. The amount of money I needed to save seemed like a huge chunk of my paycheck, especially after I accounted for money committed to taxes and tithing. I just couldn't do it! Karen and I talked about just doing 8 percent, since we'd managed that before. Even at that rate, I hit a psychological wall.

It has occurred to me in the last decade or so with the 401(k), I'd never agonized over the amount I'd been saving. It was gone before I ever saw it—deducted from my paycheck along with taxes, insurance premiums and medical savings. With electronic deposit of my paycheck, I never held crispy, green currency; it was electrons in, electrons out. Only my paystub knew the true story.

Thinking about how "out of sight, out of mind" impacts behavior, I recall using this technique before, in a slightly different fashion, when we wanted to get out of debt. At the time, we had balances on credit cards, store charge cards, auto loans, and a home equity loan. All those payments ate up a substantial portion of our take-home pay. Our "snowball" method of debt-reduction began with paying off the smallest debt first. Once that was taken care of, we didn't just spend the extra money; instead, we applied the amount of that payment to the next smallest debt. Once the second debt was paid, we took the amount we were paying for debts #1 and #2 and applied those funds to the third debt. Our payment amounts grew like a snowball rolling down a hill until we'd paid off the last consumer loan. The key was that the "extra" money didn't get a chance to be absorbed into our discretionary spending. In a way, we used "out of sight, out of mind" to fool ourselves into continuing to live as if our cash flow wasn't increasing. As a result, we got out of debt more quickly and with a lot less pain.

I'd love to go on autopilot with lots of other things I find hard to get done—things like changing the oil in our cars, replacing the filters in our furnace, adding salt to the water softener, and so on. The best way I've found to stay on top of these things is to enter them as a "recurring event" in the calendar on my phone. Even with that, I'm not as consistent as I would like to be. Other financial priorities, however, can be met with the "set it and forget it" method. Each paycheck can be direct-deposited and, at some financial institutions, split up among several accounts such as savings, an emergency fund, a car replacement fund, Christmas club, and vacation club. Regular bills can be paid through automatic online payments. Retirement and investment accounts can even be set up to regularly and automatically rebalance the investment portfolio. We already use several of these financial tools, and they certainly make life simpler.

That's why I strongly recommend automatic deductions for retirement. This "out of sight, out of mind" savings discipline is relatively painless. It's a behavioral *change that takes away the routine decision-making questions. I don't have to ask myself if I should do it or want to do it—it just happens. And I look forward to each IRA statement. I know that I can check the balance with happy surprise and say "Wow! that's a lot. And I didn't feel a thing!"*

—◊—

When you studied poetry in English class, you may have come across John Greenleaf Whittier, a nineteenth-century New Englander who is best remembered for a single couplet he penned in 1856. The two lines, which can be found in the poem *Maud Muller*, are as follows:

> *For all the sad words of tongue or pen,*
> *The saddest are these: "It might have been.*

"It might have been." These are words that are too often spoken about money matters, and they're usually spoken with a tinge of regret. Far too many people wonder how much better their lives would be if they had only started planning sooner. But you don't have to be one of those people. Instead, you can begin working your financial plan today. Not tomorrow. Not next week. Not after the first of the year. Today. Whether you feel like it, or not.

## A FEW MORE THOUGHTS ABOUT GETTING STARTED TODAY

*The secret of getting ahead
is getting started.*

MARK TWAIN

*There is no moment like the present.
The person who will not execute
his resolutions when they are
fresh upon him can have
no hope from them afterwards.*

MARIA EDGEWORTH

*Never mistake motion for action.*

ERNEST HEMINGWAY

*You must do the thing*
*you think you cannot do.*

ELEANOR ROOSEVELT


*I leave this rule for others*
*when I'm dead.*
*Be always sure you're right,*
*then go ahead."*

DAVY CROCKETT


*The most important history*
*is the history we make today.*

HENRY FORD


*Do not wait; the time will never be "just right."*
*Start where you stand, and work*
*with whatever tools you may have*
*at your command. Better tools*
*will be found as you go along.*

NAPOLEON HILL


*If I had my career over again?*
*Maybe I'd say to myself,*
*speed it up a little.*

JIMMY STEWART

# 6

## THE QUESTION

On numerous occasions, I've tried
to get my financial house in order.
I was able to stick to my budget
for a month or two, but before long I was
back to my old ways. What should I do?

## THE ANSWER

Simply put, you must pick yourself up,
dust yourself off, and try again.
You should not let past failures—
or temporary setbacks—destroy
your resolve or diminish
your self-confidence.

*You may have to fight a battle
more than once to win it.*

MARGARET THATCHER

**Stress-Busting Strategy #6**

# HAVE A STICK-TO-THE-PLAN MENTALITY

*Be like a postage stamp:*
*stick to one thing till you get there.*

JOSH BILLINGS

In 1840, an American educator named Robert H. Palmer published a book entitled *Teacher's Manual*. In it, Palmer composed a simple couplet that was intended to encourage schoolchildren to do their homework:

> *'Tis a lesson you should heed, try, try again.*
> *If at first you don't succeed, try, try again.*

That message, which most certainly applies to schoolkids of every generation, also applies to you.

Perseverance pays, especially when it comes to matters of life and debt.

As you make your way through life, you will undoubtedly experience your fair share of disappointments, detours, false starts, and outright flops. Whenever you encounter one of life's inevitable dead ends, you can be sure that you're facing a test of character. So the question of the day is not *if* you'll be tested; it's *how you will respond*. Will you give in and give up, or will you "try, try again?" The answer to this simple question will, in all probability, determine whether or not you accomplish your goals. If you keep trying, you'll eventually hit the mark, or come close. But if you give up at the first sign of failure, you'll never know how successful you might have been if you'd tried just one more time.

Formulating your financial plan is a straightforward exercise that can completed in a few hours if you work efficiently. But implementing your plan will take years, so you'll need to stay positive, and you'll need to be disciplined.

When Karen taught middle-school math, she made sure that one aspect of her classroom remained unchanged from year to year. It was a homemade poster with the following equation:

# ABILITY
## + ATTITUDE
## + PERSEVERANCE
## = SUCCESS.

That faded poster wasn't the prettiest part of the classroom décor, but it may have been the most significant. The message to math students was clear, but the formula wasn't simply a recipe for comprehending algebra, geometry, or trig. It's was also a formula that was intended for use outside the classroom. And, it's exactly what a couple needs as they put a financial plan into action. If you want to turn your dreams into reality, you'll need ability, attitude, and perseverance.

## ABILITY

*You are the only person on earth
who can use your ability.*

ZIG ZIGLAR

Some people are gifted financial managers and other people aren't. Some folks are naturally gifted with the ability to understand the mathematics and to manage the details of their finances with ease. But many people—perhaps most people—don't have that gift. As financial coaches, we encounter a few people who possess an instinctive understanding of money management; they seem born with the ability to budget, to plan, to set goals, and to succeed. But most of the people we encounter don't fit that description . . . *yet*.

Managing money is a skill that can be learned. In fact, elementary-school curriculum covers just about all the math you'll ever need to balance your budget. If you can do addition, subtraction, multiplication, and division, you have all the math skills that are required for the job. So what else do you need? You'll probably need a few more tools to place in your money-management toolkit. This book is one of those tools, but we suggest that you add a few more. Here are a few resources that come to mind for us: you can attend classes at your own church or at another neighborhood church; you can consult your parents (if they're good money managers); you can visit your local credit union and ask for assistance; you can watch online seminars and videos (we strongly suggest free online services only); or you can find respected financial coaches or counselors and listen to their podcasts or read their books (we suggest well-known authors like Larry Burkett, Dave Ramsey, Mary Hunt, or Ron Blue).

Thankfully, the lessons required to become a savvy money manager aren't overly complicated. You can learn everything you need to know, and the sooner you do, the sooner you'll begin raising your bank balance and lowering your stress level.

We believe that God has lessons that he's trying to teach all of us. And, He doesn't give up. He just keeps teaching—whether we like it or not—until we learn. Every new experience, whether good or bad, is yet another opportunity to learn something. Our challenge, then, is to discern God's lessons as quickly as we can, whether we learn them from a book, from a seminar, from a mentor, or from the experiences of everyday life. The sooner we learn those lessons, the sooner our Creator can move on to the next lesson and the next and the next.

> *How patiently God works to teach.*
> *How long He waits for us*
> *to learn the lesson.*
>
> JOHN RUSKIN

# ATTITUDE

*Ability is what you're capable of doing.*
*Motivation determines what you do.*
*Attitude determines how well you do it.*

LOU HOLTZ

There's an old saying that attitude determines altitude. How true. When we're feeling good, and when we're optimistic about the future, it's easier to hop out of bed, go to work, and strive to achieve our goals. But when Old Man Trouble pays an unexpected visit, it becomes harder to maintain a positive attitude.

If we find ourselves stuck in a financial quagmire, we may be overcome by anger and frustration. Our frustrations may lead to negative attitudes at home, and our conversations may be laced with bitterness as we complain or seek to lay blame. To arrive at the place where we can effectively work our financial plan, we must develop a positive attitude. One way to make a quick shift is to be intentionally grateful. We should, quite literally, count our blessings. Hans Selye, a pioneer of stress studies, called gratitude "the healthiest of human emotions." Gratitude transforms attitudes! But sometimes, grateful thoughts are hard to find and even harder to keep.

For most of us, life is busy and complicated. We have countless responsibilities, some of which begin before sunrise and many of which end long after sunset. Amid the crush of the daily grind, we may lose sight of God's blessings. If we ignore those blessings, we suffer. But, if we take time each day to thank the Creator for his gifts, we experience His presence, His peace, and His joy. Then, with gratitude in our hearts, we can face our financial responsibilities with the perspective and power that only He can provide.

*The things we think are
the things that feed
our souls. If we think on pure
and lovely things,
we shall grow pure
and lovely like them;
and the converse is equally true.*

HANNAH WHITALL SMITH

*The greatest day in your life and mine is when
we take total responsibility for our attitudes.
That's the day we truly grow up.*

*Each of us makes his own weather.*

## PERSEVERANCE

*Perhaps perseverance
has been the radical principle
of every truly great character.*

Perhaps the hardest part of any realistic financial plan is the fact that it takes time, lots of it. For most of us, achieving financial security isn't easy, and it's not quick. What's required is perseverance.

We've seen it time and time again. When people persevere, they succeed. This brings to mind an old folk tale called "The Frog Who Stirred the Cream." In this story, two frogs fall into a bowl of cream.

Sadly, one frog gives up and drowns, but the other frog proclaims, "I can't get out, but I won't give in!" So, he swims and struggles and kicks and flops around until he churns the cream into butter. Then, the persistent frog happily hops out. The moral of the story is this: "If you can't get out, keep swimming." That frog got out of his mess, and so can you. He had optimism; he acted bravely; and, he kept at it until—surprise—success!

Even in a down economy, we see families overcome very difficult financial circumstances. They create a plan and they work the plan. By doing so, they gain control, direction, and hope. These families— the successful ones—don't give in at the first sign of trouble, and they don't give up when confronted with the first setback. Instead, they persevere and ultimately they succeed. Then, having crossed the finish line and accomplished their goal, they're free to take a stress-reducing break and splurge just a little. Splurging can take many forms. For Ken, a Leatherman Multi-Tool sounds nice. For Karen, an armload of fat-quarters from the fabric store sounds much more relaxing. So what's your mini-splurge? And, when do you plan to earn it?

## A FEW MORE THOUGHTS
## ABOUT STICKING TO THE PLAN

*Patience and diligence,*
*like faith, remove mountains.*

WILLIAM PENN

*People aren't born to be failures.*
*Those who quietly persevere*
*always have a chance.*

JIMMY STEWART

*Perseverance is not a passive*
*submission to circumstances—*
*it is a strong and active response*
*to the difficult events of life.*

ELIZABETH GEORGE

*Success actually becomes
a habit through the
determined overcoming
of obstacles as we
meet them one by one.*

LAURA INGALLS WILDER


*No amount of falls will really
undo us if we keep picking
ourselves up after each one.*

C. S. LEWIS


*By perseverance the snail reached the ark.*

C. H. SPURGEON


*Never be afraid to recreate yourself.*

GEORGE FOREMAN

# 7

## THE QUESTION

I've done the math, and I'm not earning
enough to make ends meet. And I certainly
don't have enough money left over
to save anything. So what should I do?

## THE ANSWER

For starters, you may need to improve your skills.
Or you may need to change jobs. Or, in some
cases, you may even need to change careers.
These kinds of life-altering changes are seldom
easy, but sometimes they're required.

*In a time of drastic change,
it is the learners who inherit the future.*

ERIC HOFFER

*Life is a succession of readjustments.*

ELIZABETH BOWEN

## Stress-Busting Strategy #7

# MAXIMIZE YOUR EARNING POTENTIAL

*If I were to wish for anything,*
*I should not wish for wealth and power,*
*but for the passionate sense*
*of the potential, for the eye which,*
*ever young and ardent, sees what is possible.*

SØREN KIERKEGAARD

I don't make enough money to save *anything*." It's a complaint that we hear quite often. Here in the twenty-first century, too many people are living in a high-cost world while working at low-paying jobs. If you find yourself in this group, it's time to begin considering your options and planning for better days.

Those better days will arrive when you figure out a way, or ways, to maximize your earning potential.

An important element in achieving financial security is learning what to do with the talents God has given you. All of us have special talents and unique opportunities; you are no exception. But your talent is no guarantee of success; it must be cultivated and nurtured; otherwise, it will go unused.

In the book of Matthew, Jesus tells the parable of the talents. In it, He describes a master who leaves his servants with varying amounts of money (talents). When the master returns, some servants have put their money to work and earned more, to which the master responds, "Well done, good and faithful servant! You have been faithful with a few things; I will put you in charge of many things. Come and share your master's happiness!" (Matthew 25:21 NIV).

But the story does not end so happily for the foolish servant who was given a single talent but did nothing with it. For this man, the master had nothing but reproach: "You wicked, lazy servant!" (Matthew 25:26 NIV). The message from Jesus is clear: we must use our talents, not waste them.

Your particular talent is a treasure on temporary loan from your Creator. He intends for you to use your skill set to enrich the world and enrich your life. We encourage you to value the gift that God has given you, to nourish it, to make it grow, and to share it with the world. When you do, you'll have the satisfaction of knowing that you've made the world a better place by using abilities and opportunities that are uniquely yours.

So here's a big question for you: Is your current job *really* utilizing your God-given talents, or are you just marking time in a job that's underutilizing your abilities? If your current career is perfect for you—if your talents are maxing out and your skills are being well used—congratulations. You can skip to the next chapter. But, if your career isn't what it should be or could be, perhaps you should have a heart-to-heart talk with a very important person: the person you see every time you look in the mirror.

## THERE'S MORE THAN ONE WAY TO MOVE UP THE LADDER

If you hate your job or disrespect the leadership of the company you work for, you're probably already planning your escape to a better career. And that's good because life is simply too short to spend the rest of your life working at a job you detest. But what if you actually enjoy your work? Then, the decision isn't quite so simple. Here are a few scenarios to consider:

## Scenario #1: You Work for a Large Organization with Opportunities for Advancement

If you're working for a big company that has a multitude of job opportunities with many rungs on the corporate ladder, you can talk to your boss or to the HR person and tell her that you'd like to improve your skills and move up in the organization. Then, you can ask for feedback about ways that you can increase your value to the company. We suggest that this conversation focus not on your need for more money (your boss already knows that), but instead on ways to maximize your value to the organization. Since you're not angling for an immediate pay raise, but instead for a roadmap to a better-paying job within the organization, this meeting shouldn't be confrontational; it should be informational. After you've spoken with your supervisor, you'll probably have a better idea about your future within the company.

Your Alternatives: If you believe there's a realistic

hope for advancement, you may choose to stay put; if not, you may choose to update your résumé.

## Scenario #2: You Work at a Large Corporation with Limited Opportunities for Advancement

Some industries are growth industries, and some are not. If you work for a large company that fits neatly in the latter category, don't expect a big raise anytime soon. In fact, when an entire industry is shrinking, the companies in that sector are more likely to pass out pink slips than bonus checks.

Your Alternatives: Accept the fact that big pay raises may be a long time coming (and adjust your spending accordingly) or update your résumé and start aggressively searching for new employment.

## Scenario #3: You Work at a Small Company

If you're working for a small business, you probably have a general understanding of the owner's goals and strategies. If the owner seems ready to retire, or if the business seems to be stagnating, your upside potential will be limited and your chances for a meaningful pay raise will be limited too. But if you're working for a small business that seems poised for growth, it may be wise to make financial sacrifices now in the hopes that your talents and loyalties will be rewarded as the company grows.

Your Alternatives: If you enjoy working for a small business, but the business doesn't seem poised for growth, you may need to look for a second job. But if you're working for a rapidly growing business, you should probably talk to your boss about ways you can participate in that growth professionally and financially.

## Scenario #4: You Live in an Economically Depressed Area

Here in America, economic growth doesn't occur equally in all parts of the country. Some areas are booming while other areas are not. If you happen to live in an economically depressed region, you may have considered moving to a place with better employment opportunities. The decision to pick up and move away is a huge decision. The older you are, and the more roots you've put down in your hometown, the bigger a decision it will be. It's a tough call. But tough times sometimes require us to make tough decisions.

Your Alternatives: Before considering a move, there are many variables to consider, including your age, your family status, your current income, and the roots you've put down in the community. If you believe the economic slowdown in your area is temporary, you'll probably decide to stay put. If the economic downturn appears to be permanent, you may start looking for employment opportunities in different towns or cities.

## YOU CAN FIND A SECOND JOB IN THE GIG ECONOMY

There are 168 hours in a week. Subtract 56 hours for sleep and you still have 112 hours left over for work, recreation, family time, travel time, worship, entertainment, and everything else. Currently, the average American works an average of 34.5 hours per week (fulltime workers exceed this average, and part-time workers fall below it).

If we subtract the hours average hours worked

(34.5) from the total nonsleeping hours (112), that means that the average American worker still has 77.5 hours left over. That's a lot of hours.

If you have too much week left at the end of your paycheck—or if you're unable to save for important milestones like retirement—perhaps it's time to consider a second job. For better or worse, you're living in a gig economy, a world in which opportunities abound for people who seek to earn a little extra cash each week. And, many employers are seeking to fill positions with part-time labor or seasonal help.

Maybe you've never seen yourself as a "second-job" kind of person. Maybe you always assumed that you'd have go to work at one place, put in your 40 hours, spend a career working in good-paying jobs, and then, when you reached the magic age of 65, retire comfortably with enough mailbox money to live happily ever after. If so, the idea of a second job may seem like an assault on your self-image. It is not. Taking on a second job can be a great way to accomplish short-term goals like paying down credit-card debt. Then, when you've achieved your objectives, you decide whether or not to continue working the extra hours.

## MORE EDUCATION IS GREAT,
## BUT BEWARE OF EXPENSIVE DIPLOMAS

Perhaps you believe that you need more education to achieve your professional and financial goals. If so, you're a member of a very large club. In 2016, the Bureau of Labor and Statistics determined that over 60 percent of the American workforce twenty-five years and over did not have a college degree. Most workers had finished high school and had some post-high-school education, but the majority of American workers did not have a college diploma to hang on the wall. So tens of millions of Americans are lacking the very degree that they believe holds the potential for higher income and a better way of life. Maybe that's why so many for-profit schools, colleges, and universities are now in the business of educating, and aggressively recruiting, customer-students.

If you believe that additional education is required for you to achieve your goals, we strongly suggest that you look carefully before you leap. And we urge you *not* to sign your name on the dotted line for a heavy load of student debt.

Not all degrees are created equal. In some instances, an additional degree can make a quantifiable difference in your paycheck. In such cases, the cost-benefit analysis is straightforward. But in other cases, students amass big debts in pursuit of degrees that add little, or nothing, to their earning power. Your task, simply put, is to be sure that the degree you're about to pursue is worth the time and the money it costs to earn it.

## IT'S UP TO YOU

God's given you a set of skills and opportunities that are uniquely yours. He's put you at a particular place, at a particular time, with a personal toolkit that contains particular talents. Now, it's up to you to use those talents to make the world a better place and to make yourself a more valuable employee. The sooner you begin maximizing your God-given talents at your workplace, the better your chances of increasing your income.

Changing careers is a big decision that deserves plenty of prayer time. So, if you're thinking about making a change, don't make a move until you've talked extensively to your heavenly Father. Ask God for the strength and wisdom to accomplish His plans for you. And then, when you've prayed about it, remember this: in the final analysis, the person you see in the mirror is the very same person who's responsible for discovering, expanding, and making the most of your talents. And the clock is ticking.

Teachers, mentors, career counselors, peers, bosses, and human resources professionals can help you chart a course. So can career coaches and self-help books. In fact, all these resources can be helpful as you seek to expand your skills and increase your income. But in the end, you're the only person on earth who has the ability to make the most of your abilities. God is actively doing His part. Be sure you're doing yours.

# A FEW MORE THOUGHTS ABOUT USING YOUR GOD-GIVEN TALENTS

*Do not neglect the gift that is in you.*
1 TIMOTHY 4:14 HCSB

*It's one thing to have talent,
but another thing to know how to use it.*
ROGER MILLER

*God gives talent.
Work transforms talent into genius.*
ANNA PAVLOVA

*You aren't an accident. You were
deliberately planned, specifically gifted,
and lovingly positioned on this earth
by the Master Craftsman.*
MAX LUCADO

*Have thy tools ready;*
*God will find thee work.*

CHARLES KINGSLEY

*At the end of your life on earth you will be*
*evaluated and rewarded according to how*
*well you handled what God entrusted to you.*

RICK WARREN

*Have the daring to accept yourself*
*as a bundle of possibilities and undertake*
*the game of making the most of your best.*

HARRY EMERSON FOSDICK

*I remind you to fan into flame the gift of God.*

2 TIMOTHY 1:6 NIV

# 8

## THE QUESTION

I know that I should pay off my credit-card
balance every month, but I can't seem
to get it done. So, what should I do
about my consumer debt?

## THE ANSWER

You'll never be stress-free—and you'll never
attain financial independence—if you're
constantly accumulating high-interest
consumer debt. So you must find a way to pay
off every single credit card and every other
high-interest loan that you owe. If you sincerely
want to reduce stress and shore up your
finances, this step is not optional.

—⁓—

*Money often costs too much.*

RALPH WALDO EMERSON

**Stress-Busting Strategy #8**

# ELIMINATE HIGH-INTEREST DEBT IMMEDIATELY

*Do you want to earn 20%
risk free? Pay off your credit card.*

ANDREW TOBIAS

If you're serious about managing your money, then there's an important step you must take. This step may be painful, and it may be difficult. But it's necessary.

If you're serious about managing your money, you must eliminate high-interest debt. Period. Full stop. No exceptions.

Not paying off high-cost debt is nonsensical when you consider that your savings account is earning so much less. When Karen coaches people about their finances, she encourages them to put $1,000 in an emergency fund. Once that safety net is set up, she advises families to start paying off all the credit cards, store charge-cards, and other nonmortgage debt. Some folks resist this step, preferring to keep several thousand dollars in a savings account just in case. We understand the emotional comfort this decision brings, but it comes at a cost: the interest they'll pay on their outstanding debt. It pains us to watch someone pay 18.99% on a $2,500 credit-card balance while they earn 0.1% on the $2,500 they have in savings.

The best way to tackle short-term debt is by using the familiar snowball technique Ken described in chapter 5. You simply pay off your smallest balance first, and then pay off the next smallest balance next, and continue until you've eliminated all short-term, high-interest debt. Taking this simple step is imperative because interest rates on credit cards and payday loans are so high, and the interest income on savings accounts and CDs are low by comparison.

## A WORLD ADDICTED TO DEBT

We live in a world that has become so reliant upon debt that our entire economy depends on it. How many new automobiles would dealers sell if there were no car loans? Not very many. And how many businesses would cease operations if their short-term credit lines were called tomorrow? Plenty.

Consumers are in debt; students are in debt; businesses are in debt; and (last but not least) governments are in debt. We live in a borrow-now-and-pay-later world that's addicted to debt, but you needn't be. Just because our world revolves around oceans of borrowed money doesn't mean that you must do likewise.

Of course, not all debt is dangerous to your financial health. If you borrow money to purchase a well-located home—if you make a sensible down payment, and if you can afford all the expenses of owning and maintaining your residence—then you're probably making a wise decision. Why? Because home ownership is a great way to create equity, and mortgage debt, when used judiciously, makes home ownership possible. When used wisely and in moderation, mortgage debt can contribute to your financial well-being. But other forms of debt are not so benign.

If you're already living beyond your means and borrowing to pay for the privilege, then you know that sleepless nights and stress-filled days are the psychological payments that must be extracted from those who buy too much "now" in hopes that they can pay for those things "later." Unfortunately, "later" usually arrives sooner than expected, and that's when the trouble begins.

Everywhere you turn, businesses are trying to convince you to become their debtor. Credit cards are easy to acquire and even easier to use. And every major item in your home can be purchased using some form of consumer credit. You know the drill: zero down and "easy" monthly payments. You can buy furniture on credit, appliances on credit, and carpets on credit. You can buy lawnmowers on credit, lawn furniture on credit, and even swimming pools on credit. Want to sleep on it? Yes, you can even buy mattresses on credit. If you're willing to sign up for the debt, you can own it today and pay for it later. But you'll keep paying and paying and paying in more ways than one. You'll pay in dollars, and you'll pay in stress, but not necessarily in that order.

Excessive consumer debt has brought untold misery to countless families, and it's your job to ensure that your family is spared from this needless stress and suffering.

# A FEW MORE THOUGHTS ABOUT DEBT

*The borrower is slave to the lender.*

PROVERBS 22:7 NIV

*Home life ceases to be free and beautiful as soon as it is founded on borrowing and debt.*

HENRIK IBSEN

*It is better to go to bed supperless than rise in debt.*

BEN FRANKLIN

*If you make a habit of spending your money before you even receive it, you will forever be wanting for something.*

ST. STEPHEN OF MURET

*Never spend your money before you have it.*

THOMAS JEFFERSON

*Don't borrow or lend, but if you must do one, lend.*

JOSH BILLINGS

# 9

## THE QUESTION

Sometimes, I buy things on impulse
only to regret those purchases when
the bills come due. How can I
put a stop to impulsive spending?

## THE ANSWER

Impulse purchases can bust your budget
and torpedo your financial plan. One way
to put the brakes on emotional spending
is to examine the underlying motivations
behind your impulsivity. If you're trying to buy
happiness—or if you're simply trying to make
yourself feel better—you should acknowledge
those emotions, and then you should find better
(and less expensive) ways to reward yourself.

*There is a reason why you do what you do.*
*Discover that reason. Self-knowledge*
*is the beginning of self-correction.*

NORMAN VINCENT PEALE

## Stress-Busting Strategy #9

# RECOGNIZE AND AVOID EMOTIONAL SPENDING (ESPECIALLY ON CARS)

*The unexamined life is not worth living.*

SOCRATES

**A** car bought on a sudden whim—or anything purchased to help lift our spirits—can be a detour on the road to financial peace and security.

We didn't know who had pulled into our driveway until they stepped out of the flawlessly shiny and stylish silver car. It turned out to be a couple we knew well. They had just traveled out of state to drop their daughter off for her first year in college. As we welcomed them in, Ken pointed at the car's temporary tags. "New?" he asked the husband. With a shrug and a sheepish grin, our friend nodded. "Therapy," explained the wife.

That was a few years ago, and we were reminded of the experience as we prepared for the emotional impact of taking our oldest child to a college many hours away. We finally understood what might have motivated our friends to make that five-figure impulse buy. It happens to all of us. As we're enduring difficult situations, our hearts search for something that will make us feel better. In those moments, we sometimes make decisions without engaging our brains or consulting our budgets.

Although we didn't stop at an auto dealership on our way home, we could certainly have used some sort of "therapy" to help ease the transition. For Karen, shopping for fabric in some Amish country quilt shops would be good medicine. Ken thought relief could be found in the flavors of a gourmet fondue restaurant. In either case, it would take money to improve our moods.

Emotions impact the way we spend money. It's surprising how many financial decisions are based on passionate feelings instead of cool logic. We have an acquaintance in his fifties who calls his two-seater Mazda Miata his "midlife crisis" car. Somehow, the sporty convertible eases his dread about aging. We remember another couple whose deep insecurity led them to spend much, much more on their child's wedding than they could afford. They didn't want anyone to "look down" on them, so they went into debt (for several long years) to pay for an event most of the guests have completely forgotten about. And then there is the divorced father we met who tries to relieve his guilt about the failed marriage by showering his children with expensive gifts during their summer visit.

When we moved into our new subdivision, the deep green color of our neighbors' lawns made our grass look yellowish. For some reason, this left Ken feeling "less than" and a little bit ashamed. It was tempting to join our neighbors and chemically enhance our own little lawn. Yes, it was tempting *until* we learned that the price tag could reach a thousand dollars a year! That's definitely not how we want to spend our money. If we'd responded with our pride instead of our financial plan, we would have had more green in our yard but less green in our wallet.

Without taking time to think, to pray, and to examine our financial priorities, we're all susceptible to the snare of emotional spending. And, it's not a healthy way to spend money. Our list of financially poisonous emotions includes jealousy, guilt, loneliness, shame, unhealthy pride, fear, worthlessness, fatigue, boredom, heartbreak, paranoia, and anxiety. These are just some of the feelings that motivate us to make unwise financial decisions.

In a counseling class we learned that addicts are at their weakest when they are feeling hungry, angry, lonely or tired (these comprise the acronym HALT). Addicts are instructed to view these emotions as signals to HALT: to slow down long enough to examine their state of mind, and then to make healthy choices. In the same way, we help each other recognize negative emotions that are welling up, and we can HALT long enough to raise our defenses against emotional spending.

Not all emotions are bad for our finances. In fact, some feelings motivate us to handle money in a positive way. For example, emotions such as love, commitment, generosity, and liberality inspire us to care for our families and provide for our children. Honor and gratitude lead us to help parents and grandparents in need. Faith encourages us to feed those who hunger and to bless those in need. Responsibility and conscientiousness cause us to communicate with our spouses and create spending plans together. All of these positive emotions have beneficial outcomes.

If you've been plagued by episodes of emotional spending, it's time to look inward and search for the reasons why. Then, you can HALT emotional spending in its tracks. There's no need for you to live an "unexamined life," especially in the area of finances. You deserve better, and so, for that matter, do your loved ones.

## KEN WARNS AGAINST
## CAR-BUYING CRAZINESS

*On a visit to my hometown, we drove through a neighborhood I remembered from high-school days. The decades had not been kind to the houses on that street. Through overgrown shrubs, I could see peeling paint on several houses, a sun-faded tarp tied down where some roof shingles used to be on another, and quite a few windows repaired with duct tape. The yards were unkempt; some were littered with trash and junk.*

*The fact that the neighborhood had gone down made me sad. But what I saw parked in the gravel driveways made me mad. Parked in almost every driveway, I saw pricey, late-model cars, or high-end sport-utility vehicles, or massive pick-up trucks with huge chrome grilles. All* were blazing in the sunshine with glossy, highly polished paint. The whole scene seemed crazy to me.

I didn't know the story behind these families' choices, and I admit my flash of emotion wasn't righteous anger so much as uninformed self-righteousness based on assumptions. Looking back, I don't feel as judgmental—just very curious. As a former loan officer and financial coach, I knew these vehicles ranged in cost from $30,000 to $60,000. I'm not sure how those families made it work financially. I still recognized some of the names on their mailboxes, and I could imagine them arguing over the choice between fixing the roof and buying a more expensive automobile.

This extreme example is echoed in milder ways in my local community. Parking my car at the grocery store, at school, or at a restaurant, I'm often surprised at how many brand-new cars I see. At first I feel a little jealous. I wouldn't mind driving some of those handsome vehicles. But, my interest fades when I think about the cost. I have no doubt that behind each of these beauties is a loan with payments that will stretch out 60, 72, or even 84 months. Why do we do this? Why do we spend crazy amounts of money—borrowed funds—to roll around town in the newest and shiniest? All we really need is something to get us where we're going, but nothing is ever good enough.

*We want more. We have all the information we need to make good choices, but for some reason, we're influenced by persuasive advertising and a gut-level desire to have something that's newer, shinier, and sportier.*

*Many years ago, I stopped by a car lot to test drive an economical sedan I'd seen in the newspaper. Before I reached the car I wanted, the salesman swept me over to a sportier, prettier vehicle—one I certainly couldn't afford—and he urged me to take it for a drive. I did so, and I knew within the first mile I needed that car. It had power; it had a gorgeous interior; and it was almost new. After a brief moment of test-drive fever, I regained my sanity and said goodbye to that foreign-built speedster. And I'm thankful that I did. To have bought a car I couldn't afford would have been a very bad decision with long-lasting consequences.*

*Even now, vehicle needs remain a complicated aspect of our financial life as a family. As our family has grown, we've swapped little cars for bigger cars, graduated to a minivan, replaced that with an SUV, and now we've gone back to smaller economy vehicles. As our kids began driving, more cars were added to the fleet.*

*As vehicles have come and gone, we've struggled with tough decisions such as how much money and time we should put into car repairs before giving up and replacing* the car. With my current car, it made sense to invest in a major repair. The car had low mileage and the repair improved the car's performance. In the case of our mini-van, however, we replaced the transmission several times, sometimes under warranty and sometimes out-of-pocket. It was a terrible design that kept burning out. Looking back, it would have been much wiser to ditch that beastly purple Plymouth van and cut our losses.

Out on the road, I continue to admire the cars with sleek lines and flawless finishes. I can imagine the new-car smells and the fun feeling of punching the accelerator and surging forward with the power of a V-8. Even so, I putter along happily in one of our older, not-so-sporty cars. It's not shiny or even particularly clean, but it's paid for and it gets me where I'm going. That's good enough for me.

## PRAY ABOUT BIG PURCHASES

*Be anxious for nothing, but in everything by prayer and supplication, with thanksgiving, let your requests be made known to God.*

PHILIPPIANS 4:6 NKJV

"Be anxious for nothing." That sounds great, doesn't

it? Zero anxiety, zero worries, zero stress. Don't we all want to have that? Of course we do. But the very next words in Philippians 4:6 explain why so many of us don't have it: "But in *everything*" (our emphasis) "by prayer and supplication, with thanksgiving, let your requests be made known to God." In this single sentence, Paul instructs us to pray about everything, which obviously includes our finances.

We wonder how many new cars would be sold if every dealership had its own chapel where prospective purchasers could spend a few moments on their knees asking God for car-buying guidance? And how many people would be spared seventy-two months of expensive payments if they had only sought God's approval before they sought credit approval? This little mental exercise is, of course, a fantasy that could only take place in *The Twilight Zone*. But just because the dealership doesn't have a dedicated prayer room doesn't mean that you shouldn't have your own quiet place to pray, to think, and to ask for divine wisdom.

If you're about to make a sizeable buying decision, we advise you to slow down long enough to check things out with your spouse *and* with your Father in heaven. It's not enough to look before you leap. You should also *pray* before you leap. But don't take our word for it. You can find same advice in the book God wrote. And a good place to start is with Proverbs 3:5–6 (NIV): "Trust in the LORD with all your heart and lean not on your own understanding; in all your ways submit to him, and he will make your paths straight."

If you're about to make an emotional purchase, God would prefer that you put your credit card back in your wallet until you've had a meaningful conversation with Him. When you do, He will speak to you in the quiet corners of your heart; if you listen to Him and learn, you'll be rewarded.

—∙∙∙—

## A FEW MORE THOUGHTS ABOUT EMOTIONAL SPENDING

*Most men do not realize
how great a revenue thrift is.*

CICERO

*Beware of little expenses.*
*A small leak will sink a big ship.*

BEN FRANKLIN

*You cannot bring about prosperity*
*by discouraging thrift.*

WILLIAM BOETCKER

*Buying on credit is like drinking too much.*
*The buzz happens immediately;*
*the hangover comes the day after.*

JOYCE BROTHERS

*Any fool can waste, any fool*
*can muddle, but it takes something*
*of a man to save, and the more he saves,*
*the more of a man it makes him.*

RUDYARD KIPLING

*The safest way to double*
*your money is to fold it over once*
*and put it in your pocket.*

KIN HUBBARD

# 10

## THE QUESTION

I've made quite a few unforced financial errors that are still bothering me. What should I do?

## THE ANSWER

Everybody makes mistakes, and you will too. You can put those mistakes to good use if you learn from them, if you grow through them, and if you vow not to repeat them.

*Every calamity is a spur and valuable hint.*

RALPH WALDO EMERSON

**Stress-Busting Strategy #10**

# AVOID UNFORCED FINANCIAL ERRORS

*A person must be big enough to admit
his mistakes, smart enough to profit from them,
and strong enough to correct them.*

JOHN MAXWELL

**S**ometimes, financial setbacks are beyond our control. The factory closes or the roof blows off in a windstorm or illness visits a loved one or a Cat 5 hurricane comes barreling up from the Caribbean. These are but a few examples—you can probably think of more—of serious financial stumbling blocks that are difficult to foresee and hard to plan for.

And then there are the other kind of financial setbacks: the ones we can control, but don't. These are the unforced errors, the self-inflicted financial wounds that cause stressful days and sleepless nights. These are the mistakes—some minor and some not-so-minor—that leave us feeling regretful or embarrassed or both. These are the budget-busting blunders that should be avoided at all costs. Since confession is, indeed, good for the soul, we've decided to share a few of our greatest hits.

## OUR BIGGEST FINANCIAL BOO-BOOS

The rowdy preschooler's rough play has resulted in the inevitable—a stumble, a fall, and a mild but painful injury. After being held through the initial crying and tears, the little one holds out his chubby hand and pitifully declares that he's got a "boo-boo." As she has done dozens of times before, his mother whispers lovingly: "Let Mommy kiss it and make it better." The kiss is applied, the tears dry, and the child is off on another adventure.

If only our financial boo-boos would disappear with a simple kiss! We've all made minor money mistakes in our lives—little stumbles that stung for just a while. Maybe it was an impulse purchase of some gadget that now collects dust in the garage. Some of us can remember bigger blunders that left lasting scars—perhaps buying that timeshare that you had to pay someone to take off your hands. Either way, whether big or small, money boo-boos hurt.

As we've helped families in financial crisis, we've seen the results of unwise money decisions. Unfortunately, we, too, have made some boneheaded moves with our finances over the years. Here's a list of mistakes we've made (or seen others make) along with the reasons they made us wince in pain.

**Withdrawing retirement savings to pay bills:** Decades ago, Ken took a "lump sum distribution" of his retirement money when he changed jobs. Instead of transferring that money to an IRA invested in mutual funds, we used it to pay medical bills. It seemed like a good idea at the time, but the result was that we not only lost money to taxes and penalties, we also missed out on the wealth accumulation that would have been ours if we'd simply reinvested the money and left it alone. We once estimated what the fund balance would look like now if we'd done the right thing. Ouch! Big boo-boo.

**Not taking advantage of employer retirement plans, especially ones that match your contributions:** Ken had worked at his job for several years before the person processing payroll asked him why he wasn't putting money in the 401(k). With money as tight as it was for us back then, we didn't think we could afford to save. As a result, we were missing out on the free money the employer would have contributed to match what we put in. It wasn't small change! We started by putting in 1percent of his salary that year and increasing as we could. Our only regret is that we didn't start sooner.

**Buying stuff you don't use often when you could rent it or borrow it instead:** This is a minor booboo, but it stings a little every time we open the garage door. Sitting quietly in the corner is a beautiful and fairly expensive Husqvarna Front Tine Tiller. It's got all we need: a 205 cc Briggs and Stratton OHV Engine, forward-and-reverse transmission, variable tilling width . . . and we run it about eight hours a year. The hardware store in our town rents a better tiller at a reasonable rate. Moneywise, it would have made more sense to rent.

**Buying more house than you can handle:** Years ago, when the whole country was in a real-estate frenzy, it seemed as though everybody was betting on instant appreciation. Even before the bubble burst, people were taking on monthly payments that ate up most of the "extra" money in their budget. We didn't succumb to the real estate temptations dangled before us, but we did commit ourselves to a significant mortgage payment on the property we owned. With both of us working full-time, there was no "ouch" to this decision. But when one of us wanted to go part-time, we started to feel the squeezing pain of financial constraints. With fewer fixed housing costs, we would have been freer to follow our dreams.

The mortgage payment isn't the only thing to think about if you're trying to avoid a big-house boo-boo. If you buy property like we owned, you'll soon be purchasing things like a lawn tractor, a chain saw, underground fencing for the dog, gravel for the lane, and lots more. It all adds up.

**Not balancing the checkbook.** This one hasn't caused us much pain, at least not since Ken handed the checkbook over to Karen about twenty years ago. But as we help others with their finances, we're constantly shocked by the amount of money some have lost to overdraft fees. It's frustrating to watch smart, capable adults avoid the simple discipline of keeping track of an account balance. And it's equally surprising to hear them whine like preschoolers when they bounce a check. Even in this age of online account access, it's important to track your deposits, your checks, your debit-card transactions, your electronic-funds transfers, and other activities. So here's a stress-relieving way to avoid unnecessary fees and unnecessary frustrations: balance your account regularly. When you do, you'll enjoy the peace of mind that comes from knowing exactly how much money you have to work with at any given moment.

## CALCULATING THE TRUE COST— AND THE POTENTIAL BENEFITS— OF FINANCIAL BOO-BOOS

Looking back over twenty-something years of making money decisions together, we've begun to recognize that financial boo-boos often cost more than money. Unforced budgetary blunders are always denominated in emotional costs as well as financial ones.

If you've made a financial boo-boo of your own—and who hasn't?—you can probably attest to the needless stress you inflicted upon yourself and, perhaps, upon your loved ones. So what good can possibly come from mistakes like that? The answer is "plenty." That's right, lots of good can come from your mistakes if you learn from them and don't repeat them. Over the years, we've made our share of financial slip-ups, but we've learned from them. You can too.

Financial missteps are painful, so it's tempting to ignore the pain or minimize it or deny it altogether. But there's a better way. Instead of ignoring the hurt, we should pay attention to it and learn from it. The discomfort and the pain are signals that something isn't right. Our mistakes draw attention to areas of weakness and to the parts of our lives that need strengthening.

Financial pain pushes us to make tough but wise changes in the ways we earn, spend, and save our money. The pain also compels us to seek help when we're in over our heads. The pain motivates us to break bad habits and acquire better ones. Then, with the benefit of hard-won lessons, with fresh determination, and with a little help from our friends and mentors, we can make the most of our experiences and move on.

## A FEW MORE THOUGHTS ABOUT LEARNING FROM OUR MISTAKES

*Nothing is ever a waste of time*
*if you use the experience wisely.*

AUGUSTE RODIN

*If you have made a mistake,*
*even serious mistakes, there is always*
*another chance for you, for this thing*
*we call "failure" is not the falling down,*
*but the staying down.*

MARY PICKFORD

*A fall is not a signal to*
*lie wallowing, but to rise.*

CHRISTINA ROSSETTI

*When you blunder, blunder forward.*

THOMAS EDISON

*Every misfortune, every failure,
every loss may be transformed.
God has the power to transform
all misfortunes into "God-sends."*

Lettie Cowman

*God is able to take mistakes,
when they are committed to Him,
and make of them something
for our good and for His glory.*

Ruth Bell Graham

*Whoever who conceals their sins
does not prosper, but the one who confesses
and renounces them finds mercy.*

Proverbs 28:13 NIV

# 11

## THE QUESTION

It seems like most of my neighbors
are going on expensive vacations.
I'm tempted to take a vacation like that,
but it's not in my budget. Is it okay
to travel now and pay for it later?

## THE ANSWER

It's tempting to put that "dream vacation"
on the credit card and pay for it later—
tempting, but wrong. Instead, you can
find creative, less expensive ways to
enjoy your summer without busting
your budget or going into debt.

*Believe it or not, it's possible to
take a vacation completely debt-free.*

Dave Ramsey

## Stress-Busting Strategy #11

# AVOID BUDGET-BUSTING VACATIONS

*Sometimes I wonder what I'm gonna do;*
*'Cause there ain't no cure*
*for the summertime blues.*

Eddie Cochran and Jerry Capehart

In 1958, rockabilly singer Eddie Cochran recorded a song called "Summertime Blues." The song's lyrics tell the story of a young man who is short on cash. To earn extra spending money, the young man takes a summer job, but he quickly tires of his responsibilities. So he calls in sick. In the third verse, the young man decides to take his problems to a higher authority:

*I'm gonna take two weeks, gonna have a fine vacation.*
*Gonna take my problem to the United Nations.*

One can only wonder if the young man in "Summertime Blues" ever found the money to finance his New York vacation. After all, vacations can be *very* expensive. But they don't have to be.

You can make marvelous memories this summer without spending mountains of cash. We know because we've done it. When our children were small, we lived on one income so Karen and the kids could be home full-time. It was a great decision—one we don't regret. It was, however, very tough financially. When we took that path, we didn't anticipate how much of Karen's time and energy would go into pinching every penny.

At the same time, she felt compelled, as a stay-at-home parent, to make sure the children were getting the maximum benefit from the arrangement. She wanted to "make memories" that our kids would look back on with fondness and joy. But she faced a challenge: how to fill their summer days with memorable activities when there was so little room in the budget.

When there's an abundance of disposable income, the options are practically limitless. If wealthy parents so choose, they can sign up their kids for a complete summer's worth of camps. Dance camp. Baseball camp. Space camp. Karate camp. Overnight church camp. Then there are a multitude of vacation options: A beach trip. A stay at the lake. A trip "out west." Paying for it all is one thing, but how about the simple challenge of keeping the schedule straight? One well-to-do blogger stated that she actually creates a spreadsheet every spring to "figure out" her family's busy summer calendar.

These opportunities might (or might not) be ways to make memories for your children, but few of them were available to us when Karen was home with our kids. All the pressure was on her. How, she wondered, could she keep the kids entertained? How could she develop traditions and cultivate fun experiences with no money?

The answer, she discovered, was that you don't have to make it all happen. It's happening all around you.

When our kids, now young adults, think back to their younger years, the things they smile about surprise us. It's all simple stuff. Playing games at the kitchen table . . . Running through sprinklers on the lawn . . . Marching around the house in time with a John Philip Sousa CD . . . All of us with flashlights, making shadow animals while stuffed into a hot tent out in the front yard . . . .

These wonderful memories cost us little or nothing. But they're like gold to us. Precious.

Isn't it ironic? We have these glorious dreams of creating big, memory-making events for our children, dreams that stress us out and tempt us to overspend. We labor over all this, only to discover that the kids would have been fine just doing life with us. Simple life, sprinkled with imagination and creativity.

But what about those times when everyday life doesn't entertain your children? How do you entertain your kids when they utter those awful words: "We're b-o-o-oored"? Many families invest significant funds in video game systems, DVDs, streaming services, and other stimulating media in an attempt to cure their children's boredom. At our house, it was a little different. From the time they were quite young, our kids suffered under what we affectionately called a "new world order" of limited access to media (time limits). Along with it came an expectation that they would spend a good bit of time outside every day, weather permitting.

When our children were bored, we offered them no exciting toys or advice about what to play. Our aim was actually to understimulate them. Time after time, it worked. After the initial whining was over, we'd soon see them building elaborate villages together out of blocks, or we'd find them out in the yard making a fort out of the space under a large bush. They began to learn important things without being taught.

When we moved out to the country, these two ventured into the woods and built a half-dozen dwellings out of branches and stones, each with a specific function (for example, the one nearest the creek was a "pharmacy"). In this atmosphere, kids' imaginations ignite and the fire of creativity stays lit for hours. No amount of money could buy these experiences.

It's perfectly fine, of course, to spend money, to go on vacations, and to give children wonderful opportunities like summer camp. After our children were both in school full-time, Karen returned to part-time work and the financial stresses eased. We were able to go places without racking up mountains of credit card-debt.

We all want family fun, warm memories, and lasting traditions, even when money's tight. Just remember this: you don't have to make it all happen. It's happening all around you.

—❧—

*Children are like clocks:*
*they must be allowed to run.*

JAMES DOBSON

# 12

## THE QUESTION

At Christmastime, I have lots
of people to shop for.
It seems like every year
Christmas gets more expensive.
What's the best way
to handle the holidays?

## THE ANSWER

You should establish
a reasonable holiday budget
and stick to it. Christmas
is the season to celebrate
Christ's birth; it's not the
season to go deeply into debt.

## Stress-Busting Strategy #12

# DON'T DO CHRISTMAS ON CREDIT

*The miracle of Christmas is not on 34th Street;*
*it's in Bethlehem.*

RICK WARREN

Christmas is a season for joy and celebration. It's a special time to celebrate the birth of Christ. And it's a time for expressing our love for family, for friends, and for our Lord. But it's also a time when far too many people stress themselves out over gift giving. The result? A January credit-card bill that's still being paid off in July.

Perhaps you're old enough to remember the good old days when stores began putting out their Christmas merchandise on the day after Thanksgiving. Well, those days are gone, probably forever. Savvy marketers start selling Christmas merchandise as soon as the back-to-school sales wind down. Now, the Christmas selling season consumes one-third of the calendar year. We're bombarded with sales, specials, coupons, and a near-endless assortment of "deals" from neighborhood stores, giant retailers and the online behemoths.

Amid the rampant commercialism, and burdened by the crush of holiday obligations, we may be tempted to overlook, at least temporarily, the One whose birth we celebrate. It's a balancing act because we love giving gifts—and we enjoy receiving them—but we must never lose sight of the ultimate gift: God's Son.

As parents of young adults, we become emotional watching videos of our kids as preschoolers. Some of our favorite scenes are from Christmas mornings as they gleefully tore open their presents. Each gasp of delight and wide smile rekindles in us the lightness and joy of that moment. Maya Angelou once said, "I have found that among its other benefits, giving liberates the soul of the giver." That inner liberation and freedom can be a beautiful result of the holiday season, this "season of giving." Unfortunately, the giving spirit, when handled poorly, can have a darker, longer-lasting impact: high levels of credit-card debt. The pain is delayed—it's not until mid-January that the bills begin rolling in. By that time, however, half of the Christmas toys are broken, and the kids are already tired of the rest. Remember that warm, indulgent spirit of giving? Now it's as cold as the January wind.

As we've helped families with their finances over the years, we've seen many people who pay for Christmas all year long. Sometimes they can only make minimum payments, and the inevitable happens: another Christmas rolls around before they've paid off the bills from the previous year. We've been in a similar situation ourselves—paying bills in October for a summer vacation we'd taken in June. There's no joy in that!

There is a better way, of course. It takes some planning, some creativity, and lots of self-discipline, but a debt-free Christmas is possible. Here are five tips to help you enjoy the soul-liberating effects of giving without the aftershock of big credit-card bills.

**1. Begin with a gift budget.** This is the total amount you'd like to spend for the entire season. How big should your budget be? It's up to you. Ideally, this is an amount of money that's already safe in your savings account. According to a study performed by the

National Retail Federation, the average American shopper currently spends almost $1,000 each year on Christmas. This figure may seem tiny or huge to you (it seems rather large to us), but whatever number you choose, that's your spending limit.

**2. Make a list of everyone you'd like to give a gift to.** Your list might include immediate family, grandparents, grandchildren, cousins, friends, neighbors, and coworkers. Then there's the school teacher and the bus driver. Perhaps you'd also like to bless service providers like the person who delivers your newspaper, or your child's piano teacher, or the teen who shovels your driveway. And, how about clergy and Sunday school teachers? Your list may be short or long, but whatever its length, write this list, not out of obligation, but from the heart.

**3. Do the math and decide how much you'd like to spend on each person on your list.** For us, this is always the toughest step. Why is it so challenging? Because after we've jotted down a generous amount beside each name, the total dollar figure at the bottom of the page needs to be no more than our gift budget. As much as we'd love to inflate the budget and give with reckless abandon, we know that the result would be a financial hangover in January. A happy season of giving would be trailed by a ball and chain of debt. So we discipline ourselves and stick to our original budget, even when it's hard.

Allocating your gift budget in this way doesn't have to be a depressing exercise. You don't have to cut anyone from your list. The beauty of giving is that you have choices. And, you don't have to do what everyone else is doing. For example, friends of ours with a large family made the decision years ago not to shower their kids with Christmas gifts. Instead, each child receives a book they'll enjoy, an article of clothing they'll love wearing, and something fun like a toy, a game, or music.

Not all gifts require loads of cash. Homemade or hand-crafted gifts are sometimes the best gifts of all, especially if they're made with love. With some creativity, attentiveness, and elbow grease, you can give to your heart's content this holiday season.

**4. Choose the right gift for each recipient.** For our list, gift ideas immediately come to mind for some people; for others, we're stumped every year. To simplify a process that often makes Christmas shopping a frustrating and stressful experience, we have set the following standard: we're not in search of the perfect gift; our goal is simply to make the person smile.

Another stress-busting approach (especially when choosing a gift for someone who doesn't really need anything) is to give an experience or something consumable. Perhaps a certificate for a manicure would delight a busy mom. Tickets to a play or a sporting event might be just the thing for a couple. To a coffee lover, we've given an inexpensive set of two-ounce bags of coffee roasted right in our hometown. We once gave an assortment of potato chips (including a smoky jalapeno variety) to a brother-in-law who loves spicy food. Potato chips? For Christmas? Sure! The gift fit into our budget and was received with a smile.

Other budget-friendly gifts include personal "coupons." Perhaps you could give the pastor or youth leader a coupon for free babysitting. Anyone with a sweet tooth would be happy to receive a coupon for a homemade pie or cake or cookies. Within the immediate family, children can present their parents with a coupon for chores done around the house. A father can give his daughter a certificate good for a date-night with Daddy. Coupons for time spent together can also be very meaningful for grandparents who have everything.

**5. Be a savvy shopper.** Buying from reputable online vendors allows you to comparison shop and search for bargains whether you're buying online or at the store. With only a few weeks until Christmas, you may pay more for shipping with online purchases, but you'll save the time and fuel required to shop at the mall.

**Use a debit card or cash.** A study by Dunn & Bradstreet found that people spend 12 percent to 18 percent more when using credit cards than when using cash.

**Keep a Running Total:** As you're shopping, keep a running total of your spending and compare it to your limit. When you reach your limit, stop shopping.

**Don't open store credit cards, regardless of the discounts or rewards:** Your credit score will take a hit, you'll be tempted to spend more than you'd planned, and if you don't pay it off right away, you'll probably pay interest at a high annual percentage rate.

Our last suggestion for a debt-free Christmas may be the most important one—for next year. As soon as possible, open a Christmas-club account at your financial institution. With a Christmas club, you can make regular deposits throughout the year into an account with no withdrawals allowed. Then in late fall, you'll receive a check. It's an easy way to save your full budget so that you can pay cash for Christmas instead of going into debt.

—⟋⟍—

## A FEW MORE THOUGHTS ABOUT THE *REAL* REASON FOR THE SEASON

*The whole meaning of Christmas can be summed up in the miracle of Christ's birth.*

ARTHUR BRYANT

*Christmas, like God, is timeless and eternal.*

DALE EVANS

*Christmas means the beginning of Christianity— and a second chance for the world.*

PETER MARSHALL

*If we could condense all the truths
of Christmas into only three words,
these would be the words: "God with us."*

JOHN MACARTHUR

*The Christmas message is that there
is hope for humanity, hope of pardon,
hope of peace with God, hope of glory.*

J. I. PACKER

*Christmas, my child, is love in action. Every time
we love, every time we give, it's Christmas.*

DALE EVANS

*Go tell it on the mountain, over the hills
and everywhere. Go tell it on the mountain,
that Jesus Christ is born!*

TRADITIONAL AMERICAN SPIRITUAL

# 13

## THE QUESTION

I'm not very good with numbers, and I have a hard time keeping up with my financial records. What should I do?

## THE ANSWER

Even if it's hard, you (or your spouse) *must* take the time and expend the energy to keep an accurate record of your income and expenses. The math isn't complicated, and you can do it with a simple calculator. The only other requirement is your time, and we can assure you that the investment of your time will pay big dividends.

*Order means light and peace,*
*inward liberty and free command*
*over one's self; order is power.*

HENRI FRÉDÉRIC AMIEL

## Stress-Busting Strategy #13

# KEEP GOOD RECORDS AND REVIEW THEM (EARLY AND OFTEN)

*Organization is a habit.*

GEORGE ALLEN

In talking to couples about their finances, we've discovered an interesting fact: most of the people we counsel are mildly disorganized, or worse. The folks we help know that they're in financial hot water—and they have a general understanding of the reasons why—but more often than not, they don't have the benefit of timely, accurate record keeping. So, in most cases, our job isn't to teach them financial lessons that they've never heard of. Our job, instead, is to remind them of the common-sense principles that they already know, and to help them gain an organizational foothold so they can apply those principles effectively.

Not surprisingly, we don't have the opportunity to counsel well-organized people very often. The people who keep accurate records—the folks who balance their checkbooks regularly and pay their bills before the due date—may need an occasional financial tune-up, but they seldom need a complete financial overhaul. The people who keep meticulous records seem to have fewer financial problems than their detail-averse counterparts. And we've don't think it's a coincidence.

## FINANCIAL UNCERTAINTY AND DREAD: IT'S USUALLY ABOUT THE EXPENSES

When people can't seem to get a handle on their finances, the problem usually begins in the expense column. Usually, the people we help can predict their income with some degree of accuracy, but expenses are harder for them to anticipate. The stress of unknown expenses can become so intense that some folks prefer to let the mail pile up in the mailbox rather than face the emotional torture of opening the bills they know must be waiting for them there. So, as the month drags on, far too many folks live with a constant, nagging, low-grade sense of financial dread.

We advise a different approach. We suggest that, instead of avoiding your bills, you attack them head on and organize them. That means going to the mailbox every day, opening your bills when you receive them, placing them in the order that they need to be paid, and paying every single bill before the due date, with no exceptions.

Okay, after that last sentence, we know what you may be thinking. You're probably thinking, "If I could pay every bill on time, why would I need to be reading a book like this?" But before you dismiss our suggestion out of hand, ask yourself how many times you've missed paying a bill on its due date—and paid a late fee—even though you had enough money (or enough available credit) to pay the bill on time. If the honest answer to that question is "Never," you're to be congratulated. But if you're constantly paying late fees, you're paying dearly for that privilege.

Late fees aren't technically considered interest payments, but you can think of them in the same way. So let's say you have a $50 water bill and the late fee is $5, which is 10 percent of the total. Let's also assume that you're one week late in paying that bill, so you must pay the 10 percent penalty. In this example, the late payment has the same effect as borrowing $50 from the water company and paying $5 interest for one week's use of the money. So what's the annualized cost to you? Here's the calculation:

Amount of the Bill:                                          $50

Amount of the Late Payment:                         $5

How Late is Your Payment                         1 Week

Percentage Cost of the Late Payment
                                                  10% for 1 Week

Annualized Percentage Cost of the Late Payment
                                        520% (52 Weeks x 10%)

We admit that $5 doesn't seem like much money, but we can all agree that 520 percent is an outrageous interest rate. Of course, a late fee isn't technically a loan, so the water company can legally charge you the fee, just like the electric company can, and the gas company can, and the phone company, and your landlord can. We could go on and on, but you get the picture. Late payments are expensive.

The author James Baldwin once observed, "Anyone who has ever struggled with poverty knows how extremely expensive it is to be poor." The above example proves Baldwin's point. People who don't have enough money to pay their bills on time end up paying more for the very same goods and services that everybody else pays less for. It may not seem fair, but that's the way the world works. And that's a very good reason to acquire the habit of paying every single bill before it's due.

Once you get ahead of your bills—and once you've established your emergency fund to cushion unexpected expenses—you'll notice another benefit that can't be denominated in dollars. You'll notice a marked decrease in your stress level. Few things in modern life are more stressful than constantly dodging the bill collector. And few things in life will cause you more everyday stress than a stack of unopened bills with due dates that you suspect are going, going, gone. So here's our challenge to you: Today, if you haven't already done so, get organized. Here are some steps you can take:

1. Balance your checkbook every month (bounced checks are incredibly expensive).

2. Open every bill as it arrives.

3. Have a central place where you keep your bills and keep them organized (a file folder helps).

4. If you pay electronically, keep a close watch on the bills themselves *and* on the payment account those bills are linked to.

5. If you don't have enough money to pay your bills as they come due—or if you're constantly paying normal monthly expenses using credit cards with ever-increasing balances that you can't pay off—declare a financial "code red." Stop all nonessential spending until you can determine what steps are required to live within your means.

In summary, here's the truth, the whole truth, and nothing but the truth about organization and stress:

- Disorganization creates stress.
- Organization reduces stress.
- You deserve less stress.
- Because you deserve less stress, you deserve to be organized.
- Ultimately, you're the person who's responsible for organizing your finances and your life.
- The rest is up to you.

# A FEW MORE THOUGHTS
# ABOUT ORGANIZATION
# AND ATTENTION TO DETAIL

*When you are organized,*
*you have a special power.*
*You walk with a sure sense of purpose.*
*Your priorities are clear in your mind.*

JOHN MAXWELL

*It's the little details that are vital.*
*Little things make big things happen.*

JOHN WOODEN

*Success is in the details.*

BILL MARRIOTT

*Well-arranged time is the
surest mark of a well-arranged mind.*

ISAAC PITMAN

*The difference between
something good and
something great is attention to details.*

CHARLES SWINDOLL

*Keep thy shop
and thy shop will keep thee.*

BEN FRANKLIN

*But all things must be done properly
and in an orderly manner.*

1 CORINTHIANS 14:40 NASB

# 14

## THE QUESTION

Everything seems so expensive these days, and my paycheck hasn't kept up with my bills. I'm constantly dealing with financial stress, and it just doesn't seem fair. So what's the answer?

## THE ANSWER

It's important—actually, it's *extremely* important—that you take full responsibility for the current and future state of your finances. Don't blame other people, your boss, your family, or the government. Don't blame inflation, the world economy, or Madison-Avenue ad agencies. Don't blame credit cards, debit cards, loan officers, payday lenders, or anybody else, for that matter. Even if you're being treated unfairly—even if you're dealing with a difficult situation that you didn't create—don't look for people to blame. Look, instead, for problems you can solve and for sensible financial strategies you can implement.

**Stress-Busting Strategy #14**

# TAKE RESPONSIBILITY: YOUR FINANCIAL WELL-BEING IS UP TO YOU

*Knowledge is not power. It's potential power.*
*What's needed is the ability to motivate yourself*
*to do what you know needs doing.*

W. CLEMENT STONE

**W**elcome to the final chapter, the fourteenth common-sense principle for increasing your bank balance and reducing your stress. This principle, by the way, isn't merely a financial truism; it's also a proven prescription for improving every other aspect of your life. It's a simple strategy to articulate but a decidedly harder strategy to implement, which is one of the reasons we've saved it for last.

So, with no further ado, here's a simple, ironclad, two-word rule for managing money *and* for managing life: Take responsibility.

There, we said it. And we hope you'll take this advice in the spirit in which it is offered. We're not saying that you're entirely to blame for the current state of your financial affairs. Far from it. You may have been victimized by bad luck, by dishonest people, by shady salesmen, by spendthrift relatives, or by all of the above. You may have been bamboozled by slick Madison Avenue marketeers or by predatory payday lenders. You may have worked hard, played by the rules, and still been mistreated. But here in the real world, self-pity doesn't solve problems, so we strongly recommend that you forgive everybody—immediately—and assume responsibility for the current and future state of your finances.

Taking personal responsibility isn't simply the best way to manage your money; it's also the best way to live. And, since you've made it to the last chapter of this book, we declare that you deserve nothing but the best today, tomorrow, and the rest of your life.

## DON'T PLAY THE BLAME GAME

The poet e. e. cummings once admitted, "I am living so far beyond my income that we may almost be said to be living apart." Although we can't praise Mr. Cummings for his spending habits, we can congratulate him for this: he didn't blame anybody but himself. He didn't complain that, "They don't pay poets enough," or that, "The publishing industry is going to the dogs," or that, "Inflation has wrecked my budget." He took personal responsibility when he said, "*I am* living so far beyond my means." The rest of us should do likewise.

To blame others for our own problems is the height of futility. Yet blaming others seems to be a favorite human pastime. Why? Because blaming is much easier than fixing, and because criticizing others is so much easier than improving ourselves. So instead of solving our problems legitimately (by doing the work required to solve them) we're inclined to fret, to blame, and to criticize, while doing precious little else. When we do so, our problems, quite predictably, remain unsolved.

Because you've picked up this book, and because you've arrived at its concluding chapter, it's clear that you're serious about managing your money and reducing your stress. Congratulations. Now, it's time to take another important step; it's time to take full responsibility for the state of your financial health So, instead of looking for someone to blame, look for something to fix, and then get busy fixing it. Instead of worrying about the state of the national economy or the level of the national debt, focus on the state of your personal economy and the level of your personal debt. Even if you've been mistreated at work or misled by some smooth-talking salesperson, refuse to play the blame game. Instead, take responsibility for your finances, make peace with your past, forgive yourself for any missteps, and start building a better future.

—◆—

## A FEW MORE THOUGHTS ABOUT TAKING PERSONAL RESPONSIBILITY

*Make no excuses. Rationalize nothing.*
*Blame no one. Humble yourself.*

BETH MOORE

*Man must cease attributing his problems to his environment, and learn again to exercise his will—his personal responsibility in the realm of faith and morals.*

ALBERT SCHWEITZER

*The price of greatness is responsibility.*

WINSTON CHURCHILL

*Responsibility is a harsh taskmaster. To demand it of others without demanding it of oneself is futile and irresponsible.*

PETER DRUCKER

*Hold yourself responsible for a higher standard than anybody expects of you. Never excuse yourself. Never pity yourself. Be a hard master to yourself and be lenient to everybody else.*

HENRY WARD BEECHER

*You can't escape the responsibility of tomorrow by evading it today.*

ABRAHAM LINCOLN

# AND FINALLY:
# IT'S A MARATHON—
# TREAT IT THAT WAY

*As you know, we count as blessed those who have persevered. You have heard of Job's perseverance and have seen what the Lord finally brought about. The Lord is full of compassion and mercy.*

JAMES 5:11 NIV

As you do the hard work that's required to repair your finances and reduce your stress, you will undoubtedly experience your fair share of disappointments, detours, false starts, and foul-ups. When you do, don't become discouraged: God's not finished with you yet.

The old saying is as true today as it was when it was first spoken: "Life is a marathon, not a sprint." That's why wise travelers (like you) select a traveling companion who never tires and never falters. That partner, of course, is your heavenly Father.

The next time you find your courage tested to the limit, remember that God is as near as your next breath, and remember that He offers strength and comfort to His children. He is your shield and your strength; He is your protector and your deliverer. Whatever your challenge, whatever your trouble, God can help you persevere. And that's precisely what He'll do if you ask Him.

Perhaps you are in a hurry for God to help you resolve your current situation. Perhaps you're anxious to enjoy the rewards you feel you've already earned from life. Perhaps you're drumming your fingers, waiting for God to act. If so, be forewarned: God operates on His own timetable, not yours. Sometimes, He may answer your prayers with silence, and when He does, you must patiently persevere. In times of trouble, you must remain steadfast and trust in the merciful goodness of your Creator. Whatever your problem, financial or otherwise, God can handle it. Your job is to keep persevering until He does.

# 44

# TIMELY TIPS THAT CAN SAVE YOU THOUSANDS OF DOLLARS EACH YEAR

# 1

### Establish a Written Budget.

This is the starting point. When you gain a clear understanding of your income and expenses, you'll be less likely to splurge on impulse purchases. The simple act of creating a budget will ultimately save you hundreds, if not thousands, of dollars each year.

# 2

### If You're Married, Include Your Spouse in Every Aspect of Your Financial Plan.

In every marriage, a little rain must fall. But it needn't be a marital hurricane. To avert financial storms and the damage they inflict on a marriage you must communicate and cooperate.

# 3

## Establish an Emergency Fund.

Sit down with your spouse (if you have one) and determine how much cash you need in your account to sleep comfortably at night. Be sure your emergency fund provides a big enough cushion to cover unexpected bills or minor emergencies.

# 4

## Think Generic.

As you stroll down the grocery-store aisle, you'll notice that almost every item has a less-expensive generic equivalent. Give them a try. Even if you've been using a higher-priced brand-name product for years, you owe it to yourself and your pocketbook to experiment with its generic equivalent.

# 5

**Don't Use Credit Cards to Finance Your Lifestyle.**
Credit cards should never be confused with banks. If you want a business loan for a legitimate purpose, go to a lending institution. If you need a mortgage on your home, call a reputable broker. But if you're about to buy a consumable item on credit, be sure that you can pay for it when the bill comes due.

# 6

**If You Can't Seem To Control Your
Credit Cards Purchases, Don't Use Them.**
If you can't manage your credit cards responsibly, cut them up today and pay off your account balances as quickly as you can. Then, vow never to own another credit card as long as you live (if you can't pay off your credit cards every month, a debit card should become your "card of choice").

# 7

**Start Paying in Cash.**

Studies have shown that people are less likely to spend cash than they are to pay with plastic. There must be something about pulling the actual dollars out of our pockets that slows us down.

# 8

**Start Saving for Retirement Now.**

Even if it's only ten dollars a month, even if you're still in college, even if you love your work so much that you think you want to work forever.

# 9.

**If Your Employer Matches Your Retirement Contribution, Contribute the Maximum Amount.**
Some companies contribute a percentage of your salary to a retirement account that you own. The catch? You must match their contribution, and if you contribute nothing, neither do they. The solution? Always contribute the maximum amount that your employer will match, even if you have to get a second job to do it. Otherwise, you're turning down free money.

# 10.

**Don't Resort to Payday Lenders.**
Their interest rates are simply too high. Besides, you'll never be financially secure if you're mortgaging next week's paycheck to pay last month's bills. Rather than borrowing money from a payday lender (at triple-digit rates), you should do whatever it takes to cut back on your expenses, even if it means moving back home and living in the basement.

# 11.

## Pay Every Bill on Time.

Late fees are hazardous to your financial and emotional health. Act accordingly.

# 12.

## Coupons? Absolutely!

Clipping coupons is a great way to save money if you use coupons only for the items you really need.

# 13.

## More Convenience Usually Costs More Money.

When you drop by the local convenience store and buy a bag of chips, you'll often pay twice as much as you would at the local grocery store. Think about it. And plan ahead.

# 14

**Never Buy Consumer Goods on Credit.**
Those zero-money-down deals with "easy" payments almost always cost you more in the end. When it comes to consumer goods, don't buy them unless you can pay cash, even if it means buying used stuff instead of new.

# 15

**Don't Buy a New Car Until You Can Afford It.**
Please don't take this in the wrong way, but if you're reading this book, you probably can't afford a new car. So when can you actually afford one? In our opinion, you shouldn't buy a new car unless: 1. You can pay for it in cash, and 2. You won't miss the cash you spend on it.

# 16

**If You Buy a Used Car, Don't Go Overboard.**
Of course, you'd love to have that shiny sports car or that monster truck. But if you want to defeat stress and save money, you'll buy dependable transportation with the least possible debt (zero debt is the goal).

# 17

**Make a List of the Things
You'll Never Borrow Money to Purchase.**
Your list should include, but is not limited to: gifts, trips, boats, motorcycles, meals at restaurants, jewelry, artwork, and clothes.

# 18

### Avoid Emotional Purchases.

Are you feeling internal or external pressure to "buy it now before you change you mind?" If so, slow down, take a deep breath, and have a little chat with your Creator, or your spouse, or both. Savvy salespeople want you to buy "right now." But savvy buyers take their time (Proverbs 21:5).

# 19

### Never Buy Something
### in Order to Keep Up with the Joneses.

Are you still trying to impress your neighbors? Get over it. They're probably borrowing money to finance their expensive lifestyles, which, by the way, you're too smart to do.

# 20

**Never Cosign Someone Else's Note.**

If you're thinking about cosigning on someone else's debt, remember that once you sign your name to the dotted line, your liability is as real as if you'd borrowed the money yourself. So, if you are about to cosign someone else's obligation, follow this simple advice: don't do it.

# 21

**Don't Rack Up Huge Student Debt.**

Student debt follows you for the rest of your life, even beyond bankruptcy. Handle with care.

# 22

**A Second Job? When in Doubt, Check It Out.**
What if your regular job doesn't pay enough to meet your financial needs? If so, perhaps it's time to find a second one. After all, nowhere in the Bible does it mention the forty-hour workweek. So if you're hard at work on job #1, don't forget that job #2 is also a possibility, especially if you're trying to pay off old debts.

# 23

**Invest in Yourself with Continuing Education.**
Investments in career development pay big dividends. Make learning a lifelong endeavor.

# 24

**More Debt Isn't the Answer.**

You can't borrow your way out of debt: You'll have plenty of opportunities to "consolidate" your debts by rushing from one lender to another. These offers are tempting, but you should be very cautious. Usually, these offers require you to take on more debt, not less. And that's almost always a bad thing to do.

# 25

**Gambling Is a Bad Bet.**

Even state-sanctioned lotteries are a losing game. If you don't have lots of money, you can't afford to gamble, and if you're rich, why would you want to?

# 26

### Want to Teach Your Children About Money?
### Words Aren't Enough.

When it comes to teaching our children the most important lessons about faith or finance, the things we say pale in comparison to the things we do.

# 27

### Maintenance Matters;
### So Take Good Care of the Things You Own.

Whether it's your car, your lawnmower, your air conditioner, or your kid's tricycle, it will last longer if you keep it cleaned and oiled. A few dollars spent for preventative maintenance today may save thousands of dollars in needless expenses tomorrow.

# 28

**Quantity Saves.**

If you're buying paper towels one roll at a time, you're probably paying too much. So, if you have the space in your home, buy nonperishable goods in quantity.

# 29

**Utilize Utilities Wisely.**

Fix those pesky water leaks; turn off the lights when you leave the room; turn down the heat when you go to work. And, encourage your family members to do likewise. You'll be saving money, and you'll be doing your small part to save the environment too.

# 30

### Create a Simple Financial Plan.

Don't get bogged down in the financial planning process; you're not writing *War and Peace*. A simple budget, along with a hand-written, one-page financial plan, is better than no plan at all.

# 31

### Don't Rent to Own.

They want you to keep making monthly payments, and they don't care whether you consider those payments "rent" or "interest." But whether you call it "rent," "interest," "monthly payments," or something else, it's still money—*your* money—and rent-to-own deals are a bad way to spend it.

# 32

**Beware of the Small Print.**

There's an old saying that, "The Lord giveth, and the small print taketh away." So, beware of obligations that require you to commit yourself to a long string of payments. In such cases, the documents will always be written to favor the company that supplied the small print you're about to sign.

# 33

**Understand the Bills You Pay.**

We live in a world where every company, or so it seems, is "fee happy." And all those little fees can add up. When you receive a bill, especially one from a big company, watch for "transaction fees," "access fees," "roaming charges," "user fees," "prep fees," or any charge that ends with the word "pass-through." If you can't have the fee waived, you may want to consider changing to another vendor.

# 34

**Don't Do Christmas on Credit.**

Establish a gift-giving budget and stick to it. And if you must go deeply into debt to finance your purchases, then this is your year to give homemade gifts.

# 35

**Don't Open Store Credit Cards,**
**Regardless of the Discounts or Rewards.**

You don't need a wallet bulging with credit cards. Besides, if you're overloaded with cards, your credit score will probably take a hit, and if you have the in-store card, you'll be tempted to spend more than you'd planned.

# 36

**Don't Go Into Debt to Pay for Vacations.**

Here's a simple guideline to consider as you plan your next vacation: If you must borrow money to pay for the trip, don't take the trip. And if you tell yourself, "Oh, I won't borrow the money, I'll just put it on my credit card and pay off the balance in a few months," please remember that whether you borrow money from a bank or from a credit card company or from a rich uncle, you're still going into debt.

# 37

**Off-season Purchases Save Money.**

The best time to buy a bathing suit is in September, and the best time to buy a winter coat is in February.

# 38

### Take Advantage of
### Cost-Cutting Retail Alternatives.

In addition to wholesale clubs and online discounters, there are a wide range of low-cost alternatives to traditional retailers. If you snoop around, you'll probably find thrift stores in your community that sell all sorts of things at near-zero prices. Check them out.

# 39

### Don't Buy Large-Ticket Items If You're
### Going to Use Them Only Occasionally.

If you only need a piece of equipment once or twice a year, rent it. Your garage or storage shed should be reserved for the stuff you use often, not for the stuff you almost never use.

# 40.

## When You Accumulate Enough Money to Invest, Don't Get Greedy.

High-risk investments have the potential for high returns, but they also have the potential for no return at all. And, high-risk investments are usually high-stress investments too. So do yourself a favor: be sensible and safe. It's the smart way to invest and the peaceful way to live.

# 41.

## Simplicity Is Beautiful.

It's always a good time to slow down and simplify your life. And if a shrinking bank balance is sending you the message that it's time to downsize, that's okay too. But, before you unload that seldom-used food processor at your next yard sale, toss your credit cards into the blender and push "Liquefy."

# 42

### If Your Income Is Variable,
### Budget and Spend Conservatively.

For example, if your income depends heavily upon sales commissions, bonuses, overtime, or profit sharing, don't assume that next year will be as good as last year. The more your income changes, the more conservative should be your spending habits.

# 43

### Pray About Big Decisions.

Never make an important financial decision or a big-ticket purchase without talking to God first. As Max Lucado correctly observed, "God's solution is just a prayer away!"

# 44

**And Finally, Give Back to the Lord.**

God is the giver of all things good. What does He ask in return? A tiny ten percent. Don't withhold it from Him. (Malachi 3:10).

# ABOUT THE AUTHORS

Karen and Ken Gonyer love to help people get free from financial distress. They have served as financial coaches and counselors for over 20 years, teaching and writing about family finance from the faith perspective. Now empty-nesters with kids in college, Karen and Ken live in the beautiful Shenandoah Valley of Virginia.